5 keys to success in wrestling

Learning the sport of wrestling with faster speed and better quality

Mostafa Farahdani

ISBN:9798890340214

CONTENTS

Appreciation

First and foremost, I want to thank God for assisting me in writing for fans of honored wrestling what I have learned.

I'd want to thank and appreciate my wonderful parents, as well as all of my friends and companions, for motivating me to create this book.

Mr. Morteza Ghasemi, my beloved friend: I appreciate your exceptional generosity and concern for me in this manner, and you have always been an encouragement and source of happiness for me. I do appreciate Lord for blessing me with a friend such as you. May you be proud in the shade of God's grace for the rest of your life.

Mrs. Mahdieh Papi, I am very thankful that you, as a skilled graphic artist and digital painter, helped me develop this book. You deserve the best, and I wish you the best.

I would like to thank Mr. Farshad Abbasi for allowing me to use his photo on the cover of the book

Introduction

Putting faith in the name of God, the Most Merciful, Most Benevolent

Plaudits are to Almighty Allah, whose obedience brings proximity and, owing to Him, more benefits

Every breath taken in is life-giving, and when exhaled, it is enjoyment.

Then, each breath contains two blessings, and thanks are obligated for each.

Hello and welcome to all wrestling fans:

The goal and motivation for writing this book are to develop a full understanding of the concept of the five wrestling principles. The book is written in general to aid in understanding and learning the five wrestling principles. Therefore, athletes and coaches can study this book to maximize their potential, work on their problems, increase their learning quality and speed and save time and effort. To get more familiar with and connect more effectively this book, a general introduction to the book will be given. I will always attempt to convey the contents in the simplest manner possible . Therefore, in order for the entire audience to benefit sufficiently from these materials, fewer summarized and complex words and terms will be used in this book.

This book is about the five wrestling principles .It explains these five principles conceptually and fundamentally rather than by imposition and recommendations. It enables the wrestler and the coach to make decisions based on their current requirements, situations, and potentials, and by studying it, enhance their quality and quantity parameters. The majority of this book is a guide and hint to better understand wrestling. Wrestling is a sport with many dimensions, but there are also numerous individual differences between wrestlers. As a result, expecting progress from athletes while only offering them one or a few absolute methods is not always possible. It's worth noting that the individual requirements and circumstances of athletes and wrestlers instruct us on how to act and what strategies to employ to succeed. In a simpler way, it can be said that the proper diagnosis and the appropriate solution are what drive the wrestler to success, not different exercises and persistence. The primary objective is to save the athlete from becoming confused on the difficult and complicated path to the championship. It is hoped that after learning these five principles, the athlete will follow a straightforward and specific path to accomplish his objectives. The five major concepts that apply to all dimensions and angles in wrestling are as follows:

1. Technique

2. Tactic

3. Physical preparedness

4. Mental preparedness

5. Sports life management

Every wrestler who wishes to wrestle at a top standard and in the world-class must understand these five concepts. The class and international standing of a wrestler are based on their knowledge of and ability to apply these five principles. Those who apply these five principles will surely be more successful. The level and rank of the wrestler in the fields and tournaments are revealed by how much or how little attention is paid to these five principles.

Of course, it is obvious that wrestlers learn these five principles gradually and experimentally during their sports careers, depending on their circumstances. However, this is done in an incomplete and experimental manner rather than in a thorough and comprehensive manner. It may take years for a wrestler to get the expertise required to compete at the highest level, which means devoting much energy and time and limiting their physical life.

This book may be a useful resource for wrestlers to clear up some uncertainty and save time, energy, and money so that they can continue their sports careers and achieve greater success. It is written in an easy-to-understand style, allowing the reader to communicate with it more effectively.

The first section of the book discusses wrestling techniques. In this section, proper technique instruction and the biomechanics of wrestling techniques are discussed. On the other hand, similar books on teaching wrestling techniques are abundantly accessible on the market before the publication of this book. As a result, all techniques are more or less known to wrestlers, so it is unnecessary to explain the repetitions. We would mainly discuss the implications of biomechanics on the technique execution process and how to fight against a technique. This question is raised to determine what factors cause the techniques' development or the acquisition of points in defense and attack. The science of biomechanics can help answer these questions.

Biomechanics is actually a science that discusses internal and external forces affecting the body and the effects of these forces on movement. Due to this, it is possible to discover the secrets behind the emergence of techniques through research and investigation. In addition, by learning and comprehending them, the time required to learn the techniques will decrease, while their effectiveness and quality will increase. As a result, less effort is expended in learning techniques.

We attempted to highlight the real definition of tactics in the tactics section, as well as the many forms of tactics and their influence on the course of a wrestling match. It is essential to have a thorough understanding of tactics because they are a crucial component of wrestling, their significance is constantly increasing, and they play a very colorful role in modern wrestling. Regrettably, less attention and correct information are provided in this regard. This subject has received less attention and remains mysterious, which is because the tactics emanate straight from the wrestlers' brains and ideas, according to their circumstances. This has given rise to a variety of tactics. Two significant and evident qualities of tactics are their diversity and abundance and their speed of change, all of which have mental and intellectual foundations. As a result, wrestlers with active minds are tactically successful and effective. That is why tactics are important and should be seen specifically. If I have not said incorrectly, the tactic is the strength point in large fields and determines the outcome of close competition. Therefore, to win important matches, it is essential to learn the tactics thoroughly. In the tactics section, we will discuss the definition and types of tactics, as well as evaluate various wrestling styles, such as basic style, heterogeneous style, moment style, common style, and floating style. We will discuss the various types of tactical management in wrestling, such as energy management, technique management, time management, tactics management, etc., in the other section. Finally, we will discuss the importance of analysis and the parameters of analysis that help the athlete understand the tactical aspects and take a stance on them to succeed in the athlete's tactical component.

We shall begin with the root and origin of all mental states in the section on mental preparation. The mind and how it differs from the brain will be covered in this section, along with an examination of the mental frameworks and structure. We'll examine how the mind functions and makes decisions. Mental preparedness is a critical and crucial component of a wrestler's progression, serving as the body's driving power in wrestling and fighting. We will not discuss the traditional methods and techniques to achieve mental preparedness because of the vastness of the spirit and mind, as well as the mental differences between people. Instead, we will explain to the person what the mind is, what mental structures are there, and how the mind makes decisions. We will abstain from using techniques and prescriptions to achieve mental preparation because we believe that each person's mind should be polished according to his or her own abilities. In addition, we will discontinue the use of temporary palliative methods. We will therefore make an effort to investigate the matter more thoroughly so that the athlete is constantly mentally prepared and is able to manage and maintain mental control in any circumstance.

In this section, we will attempt to introduce mental frameworks to athletes and to open the mental filters that are the basis of all human choices so that the individual may polish and develop himself based on his mental insights and, if necessary, solve their deficiencies to ensure that they constantly have a lively mind.

However, owing to the extensiveness and complexity of the human body, as well as its sensitivity, it is impossible to address all of the issues regarding the body and to describe each organ and its role in reaching the extent of high physical fitness. Since no time will be left for us to recount the wrestling's other components, explaining them would need tens of books volumes. Finally, this will cause us to deviate from our main subject. Therefore, we shall mention some internal organs and energy production systems contributing to our physical preparation. We will try to explain how these systems work so that you understand their significance. It is preferable for you to understand where and how the energy is supplied, as well as how it should be consumed. The components of physical preparation will be covered in the following sections, along with a few physical fitness tests. A table and a diagram of physical preparation will be presented at the conclusion.

In the last section, we will discuss managing sports life and learn about the significance of this critical and significant problem throughout our sports careers. In addition, we will know the significance of sports management to our athletic development and its impact on our achievement or failure. This management encompasses all four remaining wrestling concepts. While wrestlers must possess superior technique, tactics, and physical and mental fitness, they must also possess the essential knowledge and awareness of their community. Since a wrestler is a member of society before being an athlete. Naturally, athletes will receive feedback from their society, which will have a direct effect on their sportsmanship and championship. Thus, a wrestler needs to properly understand his community and surroundings to enhance his physical performance and avoid the hazards inherent in his community. In the following, we will concisely describe the sociological factors that influence our sporting lives. This increases understanding of the factors and dangers surrounding a wrestler and aids in the management and control of your circumstances.

Chapter 1

technique

What is technique?

The knowledge and mastering of numerous techniques in wrestling is termed the technical circle. Wrestling, as you may have guessed, has two distinct divisions.

1. Attacking techniques, 2. Defending techniques

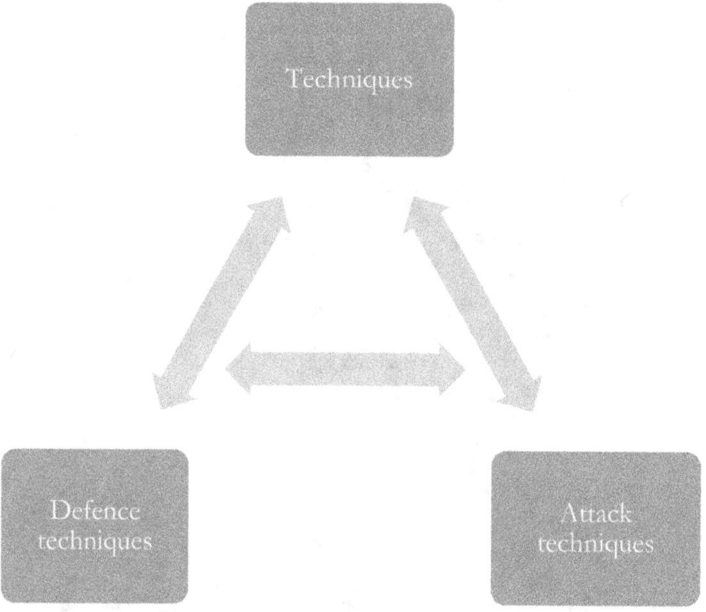

In order to attack and defend effectively, a wrestler must have technical skills and integrate them into his wrestling. Defending and attacking require their own set of rules, which can be beneficial if followed correctly. These rules are dependent on a number of factors that will be discussed later. It will be expressed in the form of headlines in this chapter, and we'll talk about them in subsequent chapters. These factors are known as wrestling tools.

What are these tools that influence our wrestling and determine our success or failure?

1. Physical preparedness. 2. Mental preparedness 3. A fighting strategy or tactic 4. Technique 5. Management of sports life
2.

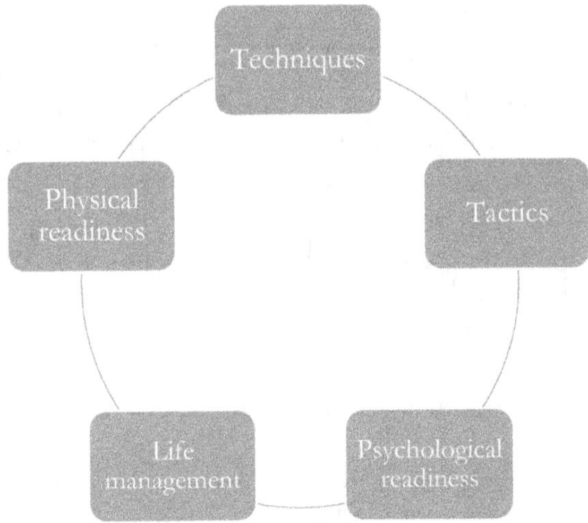

In other words, wrestling and winning are not only about having a solid technical circle; they depend on a set of factors mentioned. To be a complete wrestler, you must learn and apply the entire package of the aforementioned factors.

Learning wrestling techniques and details is an essential and unavoidable part that a wrestler must learn in an appropriate and principled manner. In a sense, the alphabet of wrestling begins here.

To acquire wrestling skills and become a "wrestler," one must first master the techniques properly and strive to grasp the techniques in all aspects. The most important aspect of the work is a comprehension of the techniques and their details because a lack of knowledge of the methods leads to incomplete learning of the techniques, which will become a habit throughout practice and require much work and effort to eliminate wrong techniques. This will take a lot of effort and time. To master the fundamentals and procedures of the technique, you must first learn a certain framework. This framework will be explained in more detail later on. The majority of wrestlers acquire this experimental understanding over the course of extensive time and training as well as by gaining the necessary experience, which is obviously a long and time-consuming process.

When it comes to wrestling, most people think it's all about combating and holding on to each other, which seems sensible. However, However, whenever we examine wrestling in depth, we discover that it is a world unto itself, and it goes beyond holding together and getting involved. Therefore, we will attempt to offer you a greater grasp of this subject and look at wrestling from other perspectives, and try to introduce you further to the difficulties that shape wrestling.

A small amount of thinking about wrestling and how points are exchanged will reveal that wrestling is governed by "physics." This is the science of physics and the branch of sports biomechanics, and subjects such as vector quantities, torque, lever, equilibrium, and stability give meaning to and form wrestling. The magnitude and quantity of these components cause scores to be exchanged and form the techniques that you will soon be familiar with.

You will understand how to deal with actions and reactions while wrestling over time and as you gain experience. But you should grasp the scientific view point to better understand their nature. It's also important to understand how to handle this phenomenon more effectively to reap the benefits and attain your objective sooner.

Therefore, one should study the biomechanics branch of physics, particularly vector quantities, torque, balance, and leverage, in order to learn better techniques, shorten learning times, and expend less energy on wrestling and its specifics.

If you look at vector quantities, such as applied force, displacement, acceleration, and velocity, which will be discussed later, and evaluate their effect on the exchange of scores, you will realize that wrestling is pure physics. To be a competent and successful wrestler with technique, you must first study and comprehend these principles and then implement them correctly. This will save you time and energy while also accelerating your journey to success compared to learning it by experience. In this condition, you should spend a significant amount of time and effort learning the wrestling principles. On the other hand, you will have less time to spend on sports, and your athletic life will decrease. You may conclude that you have missed numerous chances because of your lack of focus on the sport's various facets.

However, if you take your steps wisely, you shall reach your goals sooner, which are ideal techniques in wrestling.

Exceptions to the rule exist in wrestling, of course. Some wrestlers have intrinsic abilities, genetic, and other favorable circumstances that allow them to acquire tactics and the rest of the wrestling's package more quickly. In addition, they possess the necessary components to follow the path to becoming a wrestler, and they complete this process by attempting and ultimately succeeding.

However, we are all aware that these individuals are rare, and if this is the case, they must be trained and developed in order to provide their inherent capacities.

Many wrestlers, however, do not have these underlying or hereditary concerns. What should they do?

What are their options here? Do they have to retire from wrestling, or do they have to battle in the minor leagues? You are all aware that you can improve your weaknesses and join the ranks of skilled wrestlers with effort and practice. The most important thing is to learn but in the shortest amount of time possible. You will undoubtedly progress later if you can achieve an excellent technique and technical circle later. On the other hand, he will comprehend wrestling issues later, and this issue may take several years, causing to lose time or your sporting life to be insufficient. So keep in mind the value of time.

Of course, there are exceptions in which individuals learn about this problem sooner than without being aware of it due to favorable circumstances, such as having a knowledgeable coach or a variety of advantageous training opponents. They are capable of learning and comprehending techniques quickly and experimentally. But we're speaking about learning the nuances of each technique or dealing with a variety of techniques. We must learn how to accomplish them and apply them in any wrestling condition. As long as you incorporate them in your training, you will be able to acquire and comprehend the physical quantities mentioned in physics and have a general understanding of them. You will undoubtedly master all the perspectives of wrestling techniques if you can learn the quantities mentioned in physics, comprehend them, and have a general visualization of them. It's important to remember that you need to allocate time and resources to this topic in your training curriculum so that it leads to learning. Mental imagery and practical exercises are two ways to comprehend and understand this problem. These techniques can greatly aid you in learning and comprehending these quantities. Finally, you will comprehend how various techniques are created and how to deal with them.

What is sports biomechanics?

Biomechanics is a science derived from the sub-branches of physics, mechanics, and biology. This science is concerned with movement and how to generate movement by applying forces to the bodies of living beings like humans. In other words, sports biomechanics is a multidimensional science that studies and investigates the internal and external forces influencing the human body and the consequences of these forces on the body's movement, size, and shape. We will avoid a description of biomechanics topics because there is such a wide range of them. Because a whole book needs to be devoted to this new science, if we want to discuss it in detail, we won't have time to discuss the other wrestling components. On the other hand, we will diverge from the techniques which are the subject of our main discussion. Thus, we are compelled to ignore a number of sports biomechanics-related issues and limit our discussion to how they generally affect technique implementation.

There are two types of biomechanics: static and dynamic. Static biomechanics deals with stationery items, while dynamic biomechanics deals with moving objects. Our subject is the dynamism and motion of objects, which is split into two components: kinematics and kinetics. Cinematic kinematics focuses on objects' movement, such as displacement, velocity, and acceleration. Kinetics is concerned with the effective effects of forces, and we will discuss kinematics and kinetics in the techniques section.

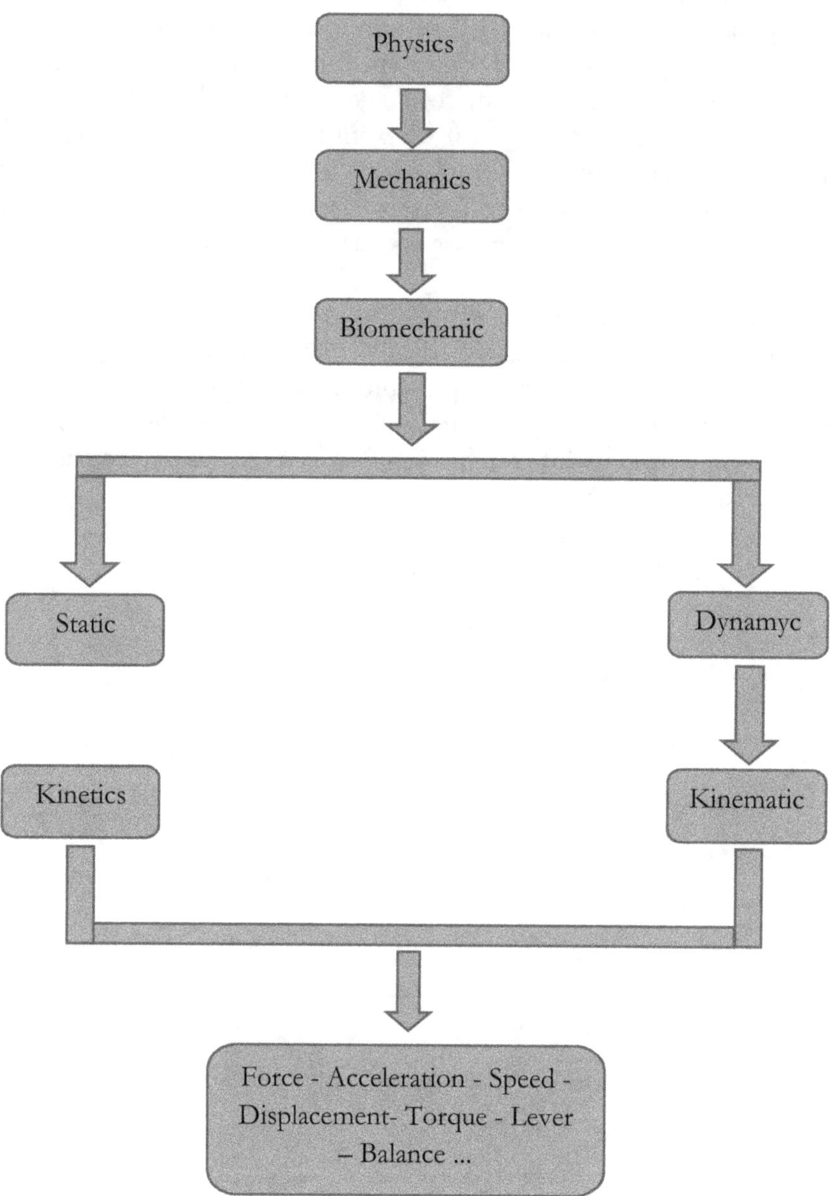

These materials aren't being presented with the intention of analyzing the field of sports biomechanics or how it affects athletes' bodies. Instead, the goal of using biomechanics is to comprehend how different techniques are formed and the way that points are exchanged in wrestling. Eventually, it is to enhance technical performance and shorten the learning period.

Wrestling is instructed in gyms by specialized coaches. The majority of wrestlers are familiar with and use a variety of techniques. Since we will attempt to address the nature and source of the issue, it is not necessary to describe all possible techniques.

The majority of wrestlers are familiar with the form and how to use techniques, but they are not knowledgeable about the nature of the techniques or how they are developed. They primarily learn and apply these techniques through experimentation, with no knowledge of how these techniques were developed. We offer these materials to achieve a better and deeper comprehension of how to implement and learn techniques to learn and be more effective, as well as to achieve complete awareness of the implementation of the technique. Because of this, you will save your time and energy until you succeed while also comprehending the existential nature and formation of these techniques.

If you comprehend all behaviors and how to form and deal with all types of techniques (which you will learn experimentally by performing a lot of exercises and with the passage of time), you can achieve a thorough understanding of all types of techniques and their variations. Assuming you have good fortune and are in a position where others can help you achieve this empirical realization. These favorable and ideal conditions will not be available to everyone. So, what should we do now? The answer is that the person should either create the conditions himself or put himself in better situations, like migrating to areas with favorable circumstances in this regard. This circumstance will probably result in additional costs for you and has its own problems.

It is necessary to explain a few things and get you ready to learn them before we can explain the branch of biomechanics in wrestling and the science of physics.

The goal of incorporating physics and vector quantities, torque, balance, levers, and their characteristics are not to teach you everything about sports physics and biomechanics. Instead, the goal is for you to be familiar with and comprehend some of these quantities. As a result, you can apply them to enhance your technical performance in wrestling. You can also use these natural laws to smooth the complex road of wrestling and championship.

Instead of spending several years in sports clubs learning the fundamentals of wrestling in order to advance to a certain technical level and gain sufficient experience in this discipline, you can also save time and energy and extend your athletic career.

You will learn the rules through the explanations that will be given to you later, allowing you to comprehend the techniques in greater detail and incorporate them into your wrestling style. You will now have a new perspective on the situation and be able to decide whether to use a technique for attack or defense.

We guarantee that if you comprehend and can put into practice these rules, you will learn a wide range of techniques and their variations more quickly, with greater assurance, and with better quality. You will also develop a creative mind in relation to all different types of techniques. It is unnecessary for you to devote years to mastering the details of the techniques and their variations. The lengthy learning process will be much shorter in this way. These rules enable you to save time and energy while also extending your sporting life and focusing your energy and time on other wrestling issues.

Note:

We don't want to confuse you by explaining all the laws and quantities of physics and biomechanics in this section. Since physics and its related fields are a vast field of study, they will not be covered in the main discussion. Instead, we'll take a closer look at some of the subjects that can help us improve our technical and technical performance in wrestling. Vector quantities, balance, torque, and leverage as well as their behaviors and effects in wrestling, are all covered. We must first briefly explain movement and movement legislation in order for you to better understand this before we can discuss biomechanics and its quantities.

What is motion?

The origin and purpose for the existence of the aforementioned quantities must be understood before we can discuss these issues and explain these concepts in biomechanical science.

Movement is the source of each of the aforementioned concepts. The entire creational system is based on movement, and all objects and particles in it are constantly moving and displacing.

What exactly is movement?

The concept of movement is related to the change of location. Movement is the branch of physics concerned with describing movement and its causes. Its origin is force, and force is the driving force behind the movement. In fact, an object cannot be moved and won't relocate until a force is applied to it.

Movement types:

1. Transitioning motion, 2. Rotational motion, 3. Rotational-transitional or general movement

1. Transitional movement:

It's a movement pattern in which the whole body moves in the same direction.

2. Rotational movement:

It is referred to as a movement when an object rotates around an axis at a specific angle. This axis can be a portion of the individual's body, or the individual's body can rotate around the external axis. Numerous joints in the human body can function as axes and generate rotational movement.

Mixed or general movement:

In sports, this sort of movement is particularly prevalent because it combines two transitional and rotational motions that are typical in most human actions.

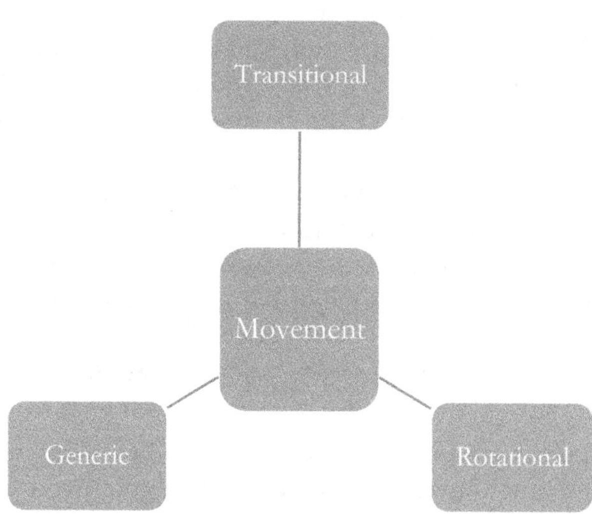

Newton's three laws of motion:

Newton's first law or inertia:

This law states that until a force is applied to an object, it will remain in the same state, whether it is at rest or moving at a constant velocity in a straight line. In other words, until a force is applied to an object and stimulates its movement, the object will attempt to maintain its earlier state and resist its change of state during movement. Inertia is the force applied to an object at the start of its movement to conquer the force of gravity.

Newton's second law of acceleration:

Acceleration is defined by Newton's second law as the rate at which an object's velocity changes over time. In other words, the force causes movement, and acceleration is the rate of change in velocity. Acceleration is proportional to force and inversely proportional to mass. Thus, the greater the force applied to an object, the greater its acceleration and the faster it will move. As a result, an object's acceleration will decrease as it becomes heavier.

Newton's third law of action and reaction:

The third law of Newton states that if one body exerts a force on another, the second body will do the same in the opposite direction. There is no single force in nature, so movement must be caused by another force.

Vector quantities

What is the quantity?

Quantity refers to anything that has a unit of measurement and can be measured, counted, enhanced, or reduced in physics. Quantities are split into two distinct types:

Main or scalar quantities include length, mass, volume, surface, density, and time; Only these quantities have a certain size and value.

Vector quantities or subquantities include force, speed, acceleration, displacement, etc.; in addition to value, these quantities have direction.

The topic of our discussion is these vector quantities and their contribution to the development of various techniques and their application in wrestling. We will discuss and assess them in the following sections. In this section, we will refrain from describing the scalar quantities, with the exception of the quantity of time, as they will not be addressed in our discussion and have little impact on our wrestling.

"As a result, vector quantities are significant because they have orientation and direction."

Types of quantities in wrestling: 1. Applied or contact force, 2. Acceleration, 3. Disposition, 4. Velocity

The wrestling and our performance can be impacted by eccentric force and time, despite the fact that they are not considered to be vector quantities. Their function will be revealed in the following sections.

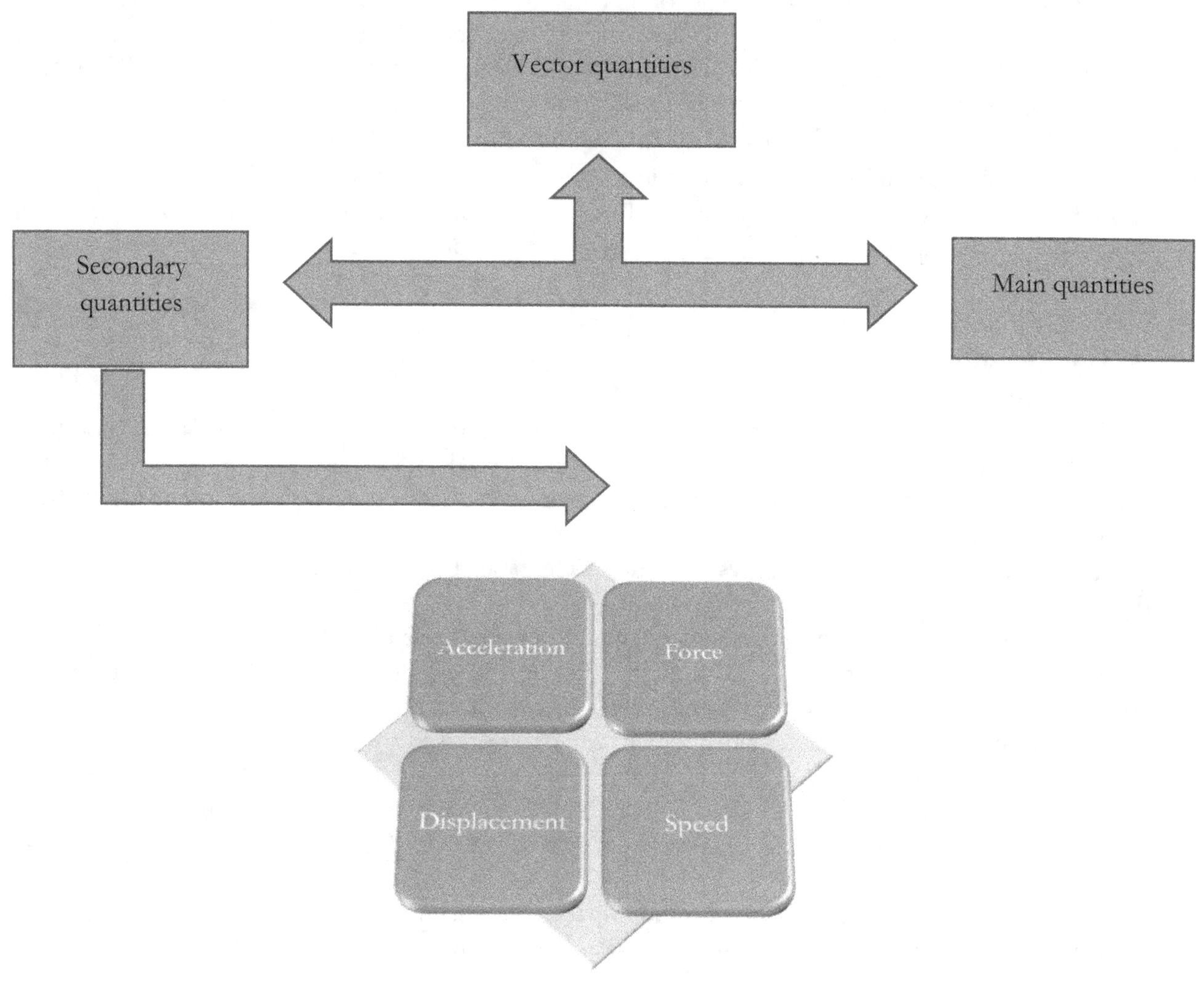

What is force?

The pressure or tension that causes movement is referred to as force. Furthermore, force refers to anything that causes movement. In reality, force is the consequence of the interaction between two bodies, which can take different forms. They fall into two groups: 1. Applied or contact force, 2. Non-contact force

Non-applied forces are not discussed, and we ignore them, including electric force, electromagnetic force, etc.

The role of vector quantities in techniques

After becoming familiar with the various vector quantity types that are thought to be crucial in the development of techniques and techniques, we'll talk about why it's essential to comprehend these quantities. We should gain a thorough understanding of these stated quantities to determine how they can be utilized.

What can physics vector quantities help us learn and discover more quickly about techniques and their nature?

As you are all aware, energy must be expended to act and move. Additionally, if we want to complete a task more quickly, we must speed it up; conversely, if we want to reduce a work's speed, we must put up resistance and friction. We must give an activity more power and speed if we want to pursue it quickly.

If wrestling and applying techniques are considered works, then the necessary vector quantities to perform the work include force, acceleration, speed, displacement, etc. In fact, the same as when using a technique or defending against one in wrestling, the largeness and smallness, direction, and orientation of these quantities determine the outcome of a work. Because of this, these quantities are significant to us in the wrestling and the execution of our techniques; more specifically, they lend vitality to the manner in which we carry out our techniques. They have the ability to make a technique look amazing and flawless, or they can make it look incomplete and unlovable. You will observe that our implemented technique will be flawed and ineffective if these quantities do not exist or are employed insufficiently. Nothing will happen without these factors because essentially every technique is directly related to them. The outcome of implementing a technique or dealing with a technique is determined by the bigness and smallness and, generally, the sum of these quantities. Since work is a vector quantity, vector quantities must be employed to complete a work.

We're all aware of the importance of applied force or physical strength in our techniques. We are also aware that speed can aid in the execution of the technique, the requirement of resisting and standing in front of the technique, and the impact of displacement on the execution of the technique. We are all conscious of the significance of the aforementioned parameters and, to some extent, understand their role in our wrestling. But we achieve them in an emotional and experiential way only by working very hard and spending a lot of time and effort on them, and even then, not in a thorough and comprehensive manner. Only our experiential understanding can alert us to the need to accelerate right away, to put up a resistance, or to shift from our starting position.

We can unquestionably use these parameters and quantities better and more properly if we know them better and more scientifically. We will also understand which instruments to employ when implementing techniques or dealing with their implementation, as well as which quantities should be prioritized in various circumstances. Consequently, understanding the application of quantities and their prioritization is crucial and fundamental, as it generates action and reaction, and scoring during the application of techniques.

The majority of wrestlers gain the necessary experience and familiarity with this time-consuming category over time by engaging in extensive practice against a variety of opponents. But with a novel strategy, by employing vector quantities and understanding them, as well as incorporating them into exercises, you can achieve excellence in this subject, as well as comprehend it more quickly and make greater progress.

Your knowledge and proficiency in applying a technique can increase if you are aware of these subjects. As a result, you are better able to comprehend the quantities that should be used to implement or deal with a technique in order to achieve success and reduce the risks associated with the insufficient implementation or dealing with a technique. In general, you will understand how to use less energy and time to accomplish your objective.

Maybe you haven't been able to understand this issue up until now, so you're going to be a little perplexed and refuse to accept it. However, the following sections will explain their function and use wrestling-related examples to help you better understand how these quantities are important to the development and application of techniques in your wrestling. Clearly, some wrestlers learn and apply these techniques experientially. However, it is crucial that all wrestlers comprehend this category and follow these issues with greater speed and assurance.

Note:

In this section, a variety of quantities will be evaluated, and an example from wrestling and performing techniques will be provided. The objective is to gain a better and more thorough understanding of how to use quantities in attack and defense. Reading these materials and visualizing them in your mind, as well as implementing them in your practical activities, can help you gain a better comprehension of this novel approach.

Note:

We're no longer interacting with an object here, and we consider the object as an individual or an opponent in wrestling.

Note:

The other aspects of a technique, including torque force, leverage, balance and stability, the center of gravity, and support surface, will not be discussed in the following examples; instead, we will only deal with vector quantities.

1. Applied force:

It is referred to as a force applied by one person to another, like pushing, which we will represent here with the letter f, and its unit is Newton.

As stated previously, force is the cause of motion, and two forces must interact with moving an object, according to Newton's three laws. This movement can now be transitional, rotational, or general.

Example:

Assume you're fighting an opponent and want to push him back. To move and push your opponent back (according to Newton's three laws), you must apply a forward force greater than your opponent's resistance force. For instance, suppose you applied a 500 newtons force to the front, and your opponent applied a 400 newtons force to the opposite direction. Since your opponent has applied less force against you, you can generally push him back. The displacement occurs because your force is greater than your opponent's. Presently, if you exert more force in the direction of your opponent's force of resistance, he will be pushed back more quickly and accelerate more.

Note:

If you can manage your opponent's displacement to the sides, and your displacement is such that you concentrate your force forward to push your opponent back, your opponent will continue to move back.

The situation could, however, turn around, with you acting as the defender. Either you must exert resistance force greater than your opponent's force to avoid being pushed back, or you must displace to the sides to avoid coming into contact with the focus of your opponent's force. In this circumstance, you should apply the so-called eccentric force, and you can avoid being pushed back by applying a greater force with greater speed and acceleration in the opposite direction of your opponent. If you are cautious, you can use several types of vector quantities to push your opponent back or vice versa for a simple activity like pushing your opponent back. At first glance, it appears to be a straightforward activity, and you have no knowledge of how these quantities are used by yourself. However, in the future, you will comprehend the significance of these quantities and their contribution in pushing your opponent, as well as the significance of these instruments in the development of techniques or dealing with them. If you look more closely, you will also notice that you have employed a variety of vector quantities for a simple pushing of the opponent back, including applied force, resistance force, eccentric force, acceleration, speed, and displacement. The combination of these quantities, both large and small, results in a simple pushi

I hope that my explanation is somewhat clear. I hope you will understand these contents, even though an issue may seem dumb and unintelligible at first. One may not be concerned with how a push is developed. Therefore, the majority of wrestlers and coaches try to implement it. Presently, if we focus on its development and implementation and comprehend its natural laws, we will unquestionably recognize its advantages and quicken our learning. In general, we will therefore save time and energy and comprehend the outstanding role of these mentioned quantities in wrestling interaction. You'll also discover how to handle them. Since experience has demonstrated that when the human mind comprehends a subject and becomes more aware, it learns better and faster and even exhibits creativity.

Look at the following image

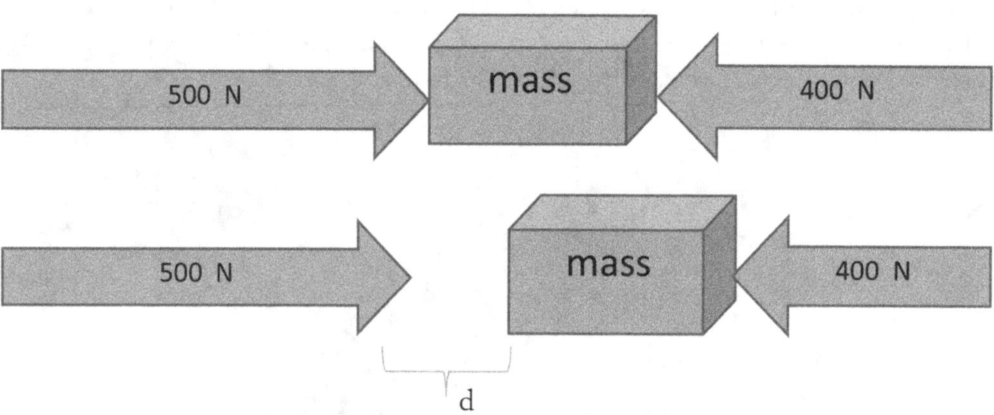

A force of 500 newtons is applied to a person m, and a force of 400 newtons is applied in the opposite direction, as shown in the Figure above. As you are aware, the force of 500 newtons will prevail over the force of 400 newtons and pull the person backward (Figure b). A person or an object will be displaced in this situation. Therefore, the greater the force applied, the further and more rapidly an object or person can be pushed back. In this section, other quantities and related functions have been ignored. The only thing that has been taken into consideration is the applied force, along with its greatness and smallness.

2. Resistance force

As previously stated, two forces must interact with each other to induce movement. Motion happens when the action's force exceeds the resistance's. There will also be no motion when the resistance force is equal to or higher than the force exerted.

Example:

Assume you have rear throw mode and want to perform it. The rear throw is possible if you deliver 500 Nm of force directly on the opponent's back and ribcage. Rear throwing is impossible due to the 600 N resistance exerted by the opponent directly in front of you (other quantities are neglected, and only the exerted force and the resistance force are regarded). Similar to the force of action described above, the force of resistance may be used to accomplish the opposite result.

However, the main reason to avoid rear throws cannot be your opponent's strength; other variables play in this situation. Displacement, eccentric force, velocity, and acceleration are some variables that will be covered in more detail later. The pressure and effort exerted by both wrestlers are insufficient to run a rear throw or avoid tolerating it. The impacts of balance, torque, center of gravity, and the amount of dependence on rear throwing are ignored in this case, and only the impacts of vector quantities are considered. Instead, the factors that determine which one is the most successful are velocity, displacement, and acceleration. This allows you to provide your force direction and size and raise or reduce its magnitude. You can also push your power from one section of the opponent's back and ribs to another, which has reduced resistance at the time. Your success rate will rise since you focus on your strengths in this scenario. Consequently, it will be clear who wrestlers made better application of their instruments (vector quantities).

And how

It is conceivable that you will employ more direct force than your opponent. For instance, if you apply 700 Nm of resistance force and your opponent applies 600 Nm, he will still not tolerate a rear throw. Using additional power and breaking the opponent's resistance force, you anticipate conducting a rear throw in this situation. However, since you overlooked the subject of velocity, time, and motion, your opponent exploits the matter of timing and velocity of movement to diminish or eliminate the impact of your acts. By completing a rear throw, your opponent departs from the center of your force (his back and ribcage) at the appropriate time or synchronization with your motion and sufficient velocity, and he is able to lessen your excess force at that point, and he will prevent a rear throw

a:

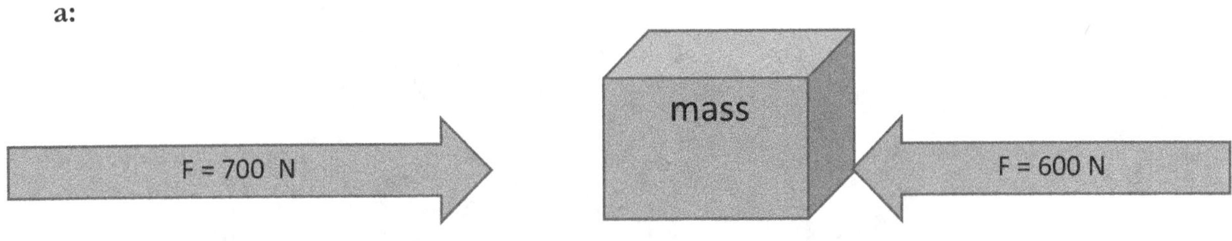

It is reasonable to expect a displacement due to the higher magnitude of the 700 N force compared to the 600 N force. Aside from that, additional factors that may interfere with our 700 N force equation include eccentric force, displacement, and velocity

b:

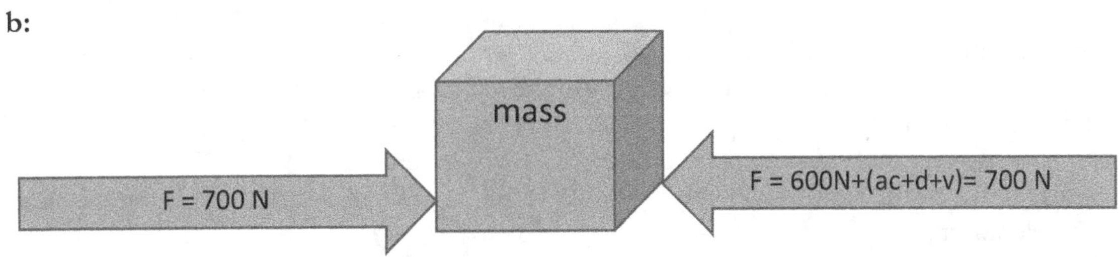

The 700 N force may be lowered continuously due to eccentric forces, displacement, and velocity.

Ac = eccentric force
D = displacement
V = velocity

This is another justification for understanding that exerting pressure and arm power alone are insufficient criteria for conducting a rear throw; other elements participate in running a rear throw. These variables have a significant and memorable part in its execution or non-execution. Owing to the great frequency of holds, most wrestlers have empirical views about them; however, they are frequently ignorant of their core composition and how they are developed. Wrestlers will now know what instruments they require to complete a technique, which principles to follow, and what aspects they must utilize if the holds are seen from the inside. These variables help to reduce energy waste. The rear throw was supposed to be accomplished due to your opponent's larger force than your resistance force. However, you could reduce the overall force of your opponent's attack by using a combined speed, displacement, and eccentric force. You will not be subject to rear throws in this case.

quantities if you intend to run rear throw more efficient.

3. What exactly is acceleration?

The rate at which an object's velocity changes is referred to as acceleration. Acceleration, signified by the letter a, is a large or small quantity of velocity caused primarily by force. The force that generates velocity is, in other words, the factor that causes acceleration.

The force is calculated using the formula f=m*a, where m represents mass, and a denotes acceleration.

By dividing the force by the mass, we can calculate acceleration.

Acceleration may take on both positive and negative quantities. During wrestling, both positive and negative acceleration may be employed while practicing and conducting athletic actions. Its regulations may be applied based on the demands of the athlete.

Example

Assume you intend to run a douk under arm sheak and go behind. According to what we've mentioned concerning acceleration, you may have greater velocity if you want to run the douk under arm sheak and go behind with maximum power. You may surpass your opponent's response strength and be more effective if you run this technique. When you use less effort to conduct douk under arm sheak and go behind, you will usually have less velocity, indicating a lesser achievement rate. Because moving at low velocities allows your opponent to respond and use their skills. This is an illustration of acceleration.

Another example is given in relation to negative acceleration. If you remember, it was expressed that acceleration is the rate of change of an object's velocity.

Consider the following scenario in which you are in the midst of a battle, and you strike your opponent under the shoulder to pull him off the mat, and you have done it with sufficient power and acceleration. As you work to push your opponent backward, you get a distinct impression that your opponent is planning to use the over-under technique. When you comprehend your opponent's plan, you draw yourself backward and displace, reducing the tension and strength of your movements so that your velocity diminishes and your acceleration reduces, and you do not undergo over-under. This is an illustration of negative acceleration that is advantageous and may aid during bridge escape. But keep in mind that you should always utilize adequate acceleration. Unnecessary and uncontrolled acceleration will raise the velocity and decrease the degree of dependence, and the wrestler will be susceptible to unbalance, particularly during standing throwing techniques. Insufficient acceleration, on the other side, will lead our technique to implement poorly, which is attributable to low force and, as a result, lesser velocity.

4. Eccentric force

This sort of force has several descriptions, which we present them as follows:

The ac sign represents an eccentric force, which is a pseudo-force perceived on the exterior of a moving object or person.

Note:

Eccentric force is an independent force and has no relationship with vector quantities; however, we have represented it as a vector quantity for the benefit of better understanding this force. Although the character of this force is distinct from that of eccentric force and the center of forces, it was regarded as a quantity to help you properly grasp the parameters of displacement and departure from the center of force as its critical and crucial function. This is essentially a resemblance and an illustration of eccentric force.

Example:

Assume your opponent gets a double leg and is attempting to make you lose some points while you are battling. As a consequence, your opponent applies 500 Nm to the front while you apply 500 NW of resistance to keep from dropping behind and overwhelming your opponent. Then, while resisting, move your legs backward and forward to execute a front headlock and leglever in the knee on your opponent. You will have control opponent's front if he does not continue to progress forward and you put your legs farther back. The front headlock and the leg lever in the knee will not execute whenever your opponent moves his legs forward with greater power and quick motion. In this displacement, there will be a debate about velocity and acceleration, with the winner being the one who moves his legs with the most velocity and power. Our discussion, however, is based on eccentric force. Assume your opponent grabs your double leg, and you apply the front headlock and leg lever in the knee while your opponent moves forward to close the gap to your feet to overwhelm and compel you to handicap. When you can flex and pull your opponent's legs to one side while in this posture, the force and velocity entering straight into your legs and the thigh behind may be diverted away from the center and center of force (behind the thigh). To avoid double-leg running, you can use eccentric force to regulate and decrease your opponent's acceleration before shifting your legs. Nevertheless, bear in mind that your response is just a few moments long and is only transitory, and you must resolve your position during this extremely brief duration. There is no assurance that you will succeed if you disregard even a minute. In this case, the consequence of an action and response on both sides is determined by your response velocity. As a deterrent and regulator arm, eccentric force in the shape of a handicap may also open up new possibilities for success. Whenever you are in danger while wrestling, it may provide you more time (but only for a brief period) and enable you to adapt to the circumstances.

If you grasp the nature of this kind of power in wrestling, you will certainly be able to establish a small space between yourself and your opponent who is maintaining the hold position. This might be significant and crucial, and you may only have a small amount of time to make the best selection. At this point, it is important to recognize and appreciate the possibilities and situations. All you must understand is which portion of your body the force is concentrated on in your opponent's methods and which orientation the force is on your torso. When you reach this stage, you should make every effort to depart from the center of your opponent's strength in the correct direction, disrupt the centralized power of your opponent at that point, and provide a very brief window of time for yourself to choose a smart option.

An essential portion of the forces via which one may understand the technique of defending against the opponent's implementation of hold is eccentric force. Wrestlers must learn how to resist hold and maintain the phase, which is one of the most crucial stages in wrestling.

Now though, you should have a better idea of what these quantities represent and what they accomplish for us. When it comes to wrestling, you employ these sorts of quantities over and over repeatedly without even recognizing them or understanding where they came from or how they were initiated. During your wrestling matches, you make extensively use of them. The point of application, that is, when and how much of these quantities are utilized, is critical. These quantities, as well as the suitable time and volume, determine the formulation and application of a method in practice. In truth, repetition is the mother of all knowledge acquisition; however, for empirical learning to be effective, you must invest a significant amount of time and energy; this is the most difficult aspect of the adventure. It may be extremely beneficial in your difficulties if you study and appreciate the same elements and integrate them into your education program to finish up learning.

5. What is displacement?

The displacement denoted by the letter d indicates the amount an object or individual travels away from its initial location (creating a distance).

The magnitude of the quantities is determined by providing distance and displacement, which overshadows the amount of the delivered force. By establishing a space, you may minimize the force imposed on you by your opponent and vice versa. By decreasing the space between you and your opponent, you may also enhance the power of your attack on the opponent (by levers, which will be discussed later). Depending on your location, you may create this space or motion on either side, backward or forward.

Displacement, similar to eccentric force, is very significant and may be quite beneficial.

Whenever wrestlers comprehend the importance of the quantity of movement, they will not overlook it and will recognize its numerous advantages and use them. In order to get free of the pressure and relieve yourself, you'll need this much displacement. Another advantage of moving quickly is that it opens up fresh windows of opportunity, which may then be used to generate new circumstances for you to encounter. So don't undervalue it. I would not be incorrect if I stated that this mobility and quickness of movement is one of the secrets to achievement in wrestling.

By moving oneself in the appropriate way while wrestling, you may view new windows and witness new circumstances, making it simpler for you to collect points. Wrestling is full of movements.

Example

Assume you're in the assault phase and want to run a flying mare. First and foremost, you must move and minimize your distance from your opponent to get closer to the opponent, or you must draw your opponent, which is displacement. To accomplish hold, you must first drag the opponent's head and neck down and subsequently move the opponent's head away from its initial posture. Then you must move your legs and spin your legs while striking.

Suppose your opponent tries to perform the same flying mare on you during your defensive phase. You may move your legs at the appropriate moment to separate yourself from the opponent and depart from the center of the opponent's force based on the force that the opponent has delivered to complete the hold. In this scenario, you are essentially contesting the technique that your opponent intends to use against you. You are creating a brief period of time for yourself to prevent the opponent from maintaining the hold as a result of the quantities. In this situation, you may change the effects of hundreds of different holds to raise or reduce their effectiveness.

Because of the quantity of movement and velocity, you can perform or fight against hundreds of Holds as long as you grasp and apply the significance of motion.

Displacement directions

6. What exactly is velocity?

Velocity, symbolized by the letter v, is, in my view, the maximum amount of movement made by an object or an individual in a short duration.

There are two kinds of speeds: instantaneous and constant.

Example

Velocity is a complement to all other quantities, and without it, nothing would function properly. The quantity and the labor that has to be accomplished are given life by the velocity. What will occur whether there is not any velocity in the hold you intend to play or vice versa in the defensive phase depending on the situation. This condition is a bit simpler to grasp than the other quantities. Your motion will be lifeless and uninspired under these circumstances, but when you accelerate it, it will be attractive and passionate. Therefore, velocity is crucial in shaping your defense or assault, as well as completing and consolidating your function.

Assume you wish to conduct a front takedown with a single outside leg. You assault your opponent's leg at the appropriate velocity, outpacing your opponent's response time and reaching his ankle. Next, you rapidly rise up from the floor and dominate your opponent's resistance strength. Then you immediately implement your intended hold and disturb your opponent's decision-making ability, resulting in points. Take note of the reality that (it is the velocity that takes precedence over the other qualities) or vice versa; whenever your opponent hits your ankle, you refuse it with your response velocity and so forth.

It is undeniable that comprehending vector quantities allows one to achieve and come to a conclusion, but if one neglects the issue of velocity in all dimensions and orientations connected to quantities, the quantities will be significantly weakened. As a result, it is the velocity of our a[...]

7. What is timing?

Timing may refer to being in the correct position at the appropriate moment.

Timing, in its broadest definition, may be defined as timely implementation.

Example

Your hold implementation will surely be incomplete if you are not in the proper position and appropriate moment. It is critical that you run hold at the appropriate time and position, and creating the appropriate circumstance will need your precision and attention to detail. As a result, establishing a chance to attack necessitates using special techniques.

Assume you wish to use the fireman scarry hold. Besides being familiar with the issues of quantities (force, velocity, displacement, acceleration, etc.), you must also be aware of the time and position at which your hold will be performed.

Generally, you cannot apply the fireman scarry method on your opponent when standing perpendicularly. So, you can't run firemen scarry hold anytime you want at the proper position. If you want to be able to exercise your hold, you must first establish the circumstances or opportunities for yourself to pass through the opponent's openings at the appropriate time frame.

Additionally, you cannot execute single leg movements anywhere and at any time; instead, you must pay respect to the time and location in which you are working. In the incorrect condition, your single-leg implementation will fail, and if you operate at the incorrect moment, you will still get nothing as a result of your hold. These two criteria work in conjunction with one another, and without one of them, your hold will be insufficient (here, we have neglected the other quantities and not regarded their role). In this circumstance, we are simply concerned with the suitable time and position, timing, to familiarize with this significant and essential subject.

What is the secret of exchanging points during a wrestling action and reaction?

Because it is important for you to be thoroughly familiar with these quantities and how to interact with them, I would like to provide a detailed instance of a wrestling technique for you to further comprehend the right examples. The Takedown hold is an integral part of Iranian wrestling; it is a representation of Iranian wrestling, and everybody is acquainted with that. Because the wrestling alphabet in this region begins with the same approach, I'd wish to investigate it and illustrate all of its facets. In addition, I intend to demonstrate the importance of vector quantities during the execution of this hold, how points are interchanged in this technique, and the advantages of effectively and efficiently utilizing these quantities. Moreover, I would like to highlight that failing to use it in a suitable and rightful way will be detrimental to your health.

I also want to demonstrate the impact of employing big and small roles of these quantities no your assault or defensive state.

Example

Assume you wish to execute the single-leg hold. To be able to cross your opponent's hurdles, you must initially cross his or her hands or the identical barriers, which necessitates positioning. You'll require to shift your feet on the mat to observe a fresh hole and vent to touch your opponent's foot. The single-leg hold is performed to assault your opponent after locating the appropriate opening and establishing the proper position, as well as positioning and supplying the essential position. You next strike your opponent's foot with the proper acceleration, which is the same as shattering your knees, by shortening your distance from him and decreasing your elevation degree. Following that, you swiftly attempt to regain the elevation of your knees to their former position so that the single leg is totally in your hands. You have already completed half of the function. Let us initially look at this 50% of the activity, and subsequently, we will evaluate the rest.

Vector quantities play a significant role in this initial half of the fight, as you first employ the displacement quantity to get the opponent's single leg so that you can create a new opening to approach the opponent's foot. Then, you start the positioning toward establishing a takedown position based on the quantity of force applied. Then, you minimize your distance or displacement from the other opponent by modifying your position, and by bending your knees or lowering your level of height in respect to your opponent, you generate an accelerating force. You will subsequently assault your opponent's foot and grip it in your hands, and then return your knees to their previous position and entirely capture the single leg utilizing the quantity of velocity. This is the optimal method for obtaining a single leg for anyone who desires perfect performance and optimal utilization of all vector quantities. This indicates that by proper displacement, the wrestler creates the circumstances for the takedown and may execute with the necessary amount of force in positioning to establish the takedown position. After bending his knees and decreasing his elevation level in front of the opponent, he accelerates and approaches the opponent's leg. Next, he can condense himself and revert to his former state with the assistance of the appropriate velocity, completing the takedown. However, this flawless take-down occurs whenever we can effectively use these quantities and know their necessity, size, and volume of usage. Other than that, we will be challenged, and the technique we execute will be deficient, at which point we will be subjected to the opponent's defensive response. Bear in mind that our opponent possesses identical instruments and is capable of retaliating with similar vector quantities and affecting our assault. A better outcome will be achieved by those who can effectively use their quantities, regardless of how large or small their quantities are.

Now consider what would happen if you neglected to use your quantities throughout the takedown.

Suppose you desired to perform a single leg but could not do so because of the amount of displacement available or because you could not offer any new positions. There will be no takedown in this situation. Regardless of your useless fight or displacement, you have been unsuccessful and cannot apply the necessary force to pass through the opponent's hands at the phase of positioning and applying force. Even if you complete these two phases successfully, you may fail to accelerate sufficiently during the take-down, and your attack is rendered ineffective due to the possibility of an opponent's counter-offensive. This position may be presented where you can assault your opponent with correct acceleration and approach the foot, but you are unable to utilize the speed effectively and climb up. In response to your shorter reaction time to get up, your opponent runs a front headlock and a leglever in the knee, and your takedown is unfinished. As you can observe, failure to complete any of the above quantities can prevent you from completing even a single leg. In this scenario, you require these instruments to obtain a normal single leg, and the degree and size of these quantities determine the outcome of both wrestlers obtaining a single leg.

However, assume you run the single leg successfully and stand up in the second 50%.

Presently, what do you need to do to get points and ground position from your opponent, and what do you need to do?

First and foremost, the time issue must not be overlooked, and the takedown technique, the second half's most crucial component, is constructed here. A malfunction to do so could possibly jeopardize the resolution of all your functions. To gain ground position and score points from your opponent, y You should not allow too much time between the initial phase, which is to complete the takedown, and the second one, which is to accomplish your technique to gain ground position and score points from your opponent. Since if you miss this excellent chance during the transition phase, you are effectively allowing your opponent to respond and employ vector instruments and quantities. During this time, your opponent can respond appropriately and render your function difficult or perhaps counteract your assault. The following stage is to execute your preferred or planned technique.

The four quantities of velocity, force, displacement, and acceleration should be used at this point so that you can potentially transform a single leg to a double leg, transform it into a front takedown with an outside single leg, or do a rear takedown with a single leg tackle, among other things. The technique you should employ is frequently dictated by the scenario in which your opponent finds himself. This interchange of attacks is greatly influenced by the four quantities of velocity, displacement, force, and acceleration immediately available while executing the technique of your choice for your opponent's ground position. While using these quantities correctly and in sufficient quantities, you will be successful; nevertheless, if you decrease their strength and position, the outcome will frequently be unsatisfactory. So, your prospective takedown will enter other phases that will necessitate the expenditure of additional energy, and the consequence will be unpredictable.

In this circumstance, to temporarily diminish the opponent's resistance and minimize his reaction strength to a certain extent and subsequently take appropriate action again, you will have to employ the displacement quantity again in accordance with the opponent's response and resistance. You must alter your execution style to obtain points due to the same four criteria or possibly due to the displacement and change in location. It is expected that interactions will resume until either one of the two wrestlers gives up and neglect the quantities until a score is obtained or that both wrestlers remain immobile until the referee calls the battle to a close at some point in this condition

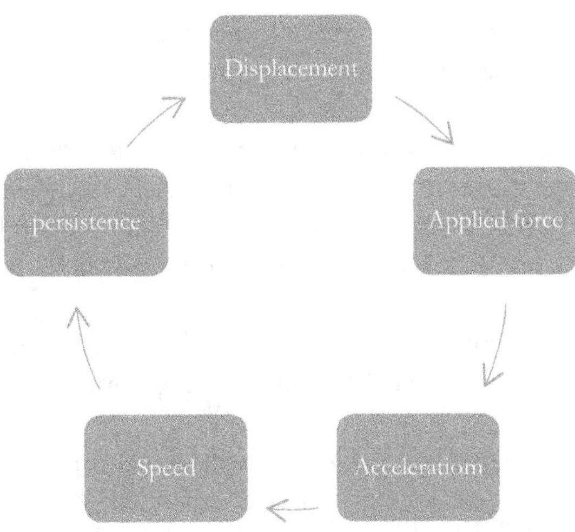

I hope you've concluded that the explanation for the point exchange in wrestling is the usage of quantities, and that it is their large and small quantity giving wrestling its vitality and generate points. Additionally, the employment of quantities indicates the presence of physical fitness variables that serve as your motivator. Bear in mind that even if you grasp the quantities but lack the means to apply them, your function will lack the essential advantage and result, as the two are complementary.

These four quantities are significant and impactful as a result of this. As a result of ignoring these four

quantities, the opponent will respond, and the winner will be whoever exploits his quantities most effectively and appropriately. Vector quantities, as previously stated, have both a magnitude and an orientation.

Note: The existence of physical fitness variables, which can speed up the process of utilizing quantities and complementing them, is the instrument utilized to take benefits of quantities and maximize their potential.

Example

You will continuously require instruments to accomplish your objectives, such as a master builder wishing to construct a house. A master builder may be familiar with all of the procedures and methods for building a house, and he may even be experienced in them; however, if he does not access the instruments and equipment necessary to complete the function, it will most likely be unproductive and insufficiently completed. The similarities between wrestling and using amounts include that understanding quantities performs the character of master-building skills, and physical preparation serves the part of instruments and equipment.

I expect that you now realize and recognize that you have employed these quantities repeatedly without realizing what you have been doing.

I hope you have grasped the significance of the fact that the magnitude of these quantities, rather than the names and customs of the wrestlers, affect the consequence of an assault or a defense on your side.

Even though writing this material is not a functional substitute for exercise, it is feasible to grasp the notion by studying it and using mental imagery, and putting the material acquired into action in real situations.

Vector quantities and their substantial function in wrestling are described as follows:

I hope you gained a basic understanding of these subjects as I attempted to familiarize you with the discipline of physics and the section on vector quantities. It is inevitable that through practice, these aspects and a mental image will aid in your comprehension and appreciation of my presentation.

I expect you comprehend that wrestling is no anymore only grappling or holding each other but concerning a collection of quantities that shape and bring life to our wrestling and involve scoring points.

"In reality, wrestling is the craftsmanship of utilizing vector quantities and normal physical laws, and anybody really with an improved and deeper comprehension of these laws will unquestionably be more successful in executing the technique and technical circle of wrestling and will know wrestling techniques more effectively and quickly."

Additionally, another definition of wrestling is as follows:

"Wrestling is the ability to employ vector quantities such as time, location, and quantity."

The science of sports biomechanics and wrestling, among other things, is concerned with the measurement of other parameters, which will be described further below and elsewhere.

Indeed, wrestling is a full collection of quantities that must be applied at the appropriate time, place, and quantity. During your wrestling matches, it should be remembered that the quantities of each type fluctuate continually from one to another. These circumstances are not always stable and must be adjusted consistently based on the actions and reactions of both athletes. Instead of focusing on one or more of these quantities, you should use all of them at the appropriate time and in the correct position to improve your overall performance. Recognize the importance of prioritizing the use of these quantities to develop into a flawless and professional wrestler in the area of technical wrestling.

Using the explanations provided about the different sorts of quantities and how to employ them in wrestling, you may currently practice simulating the many types of approaches and methods to interact with them, and by doing so, you will find the hidden message of these quantities. Through repeating them, you will be able to determine your own limitations and talents, as well as what you require to enhance your performance. Thus, you will be relieved of some uncertainty, and your way forward will become more visible.

Constantly keep in mind that two principles govern the application of the techniques:

1. Appropriate and rational prioritization while employing vector quantities, 2. The big and small quantities of vector quantities employed, as well as their sizes

We must initially prioritize and employ the vector quantities that are most important when acting and reacting in wrestling. In the second place, it is necessary to determine how much quantity is required. For instance, the amount of velocity, force, displacement required, and so forth. A comprehension of vector quantities is also necessary, and this can only be achieved through constant repetition and learning. This is due to the fact that our minds record and archive every displacement, whether positive or negative and then recalls them when required. We shall go into greater detail about the mind, memory, and archive of mental material in the chapter on mental preparation, so we will skip over it for the time being here. Simply understand that "it comes out of the jar exactly as it is," which means that whatever we have exercised, correctly or badly, and whatever we have learned, we will unavoidably demonstrate the same when needed.

Everything we plant, we must eventually harvest. We must demonstrate a skill that we have mastered inadequately and improperly or vice versa. Thus, it is critical and essential that we are adequately and thoroughly taught a technique or anything like it.

How are wrestling techniques and techniques developed?

1. Using your prior desire and intention, you choose to create the situations necessary for a technique.

2. Circumstances that compel you to react and execute the technique.

As with all combative arts, most of the performance criteria for wrestling techniques involve action and reaction.

What elements contribute to the execution of a technique or our action and reaction?

1. Adequate and suitable physical preparation; 2. Adequate attitude and self-confidence; 3. Adequate and acceptable technical competence. 4. Suitable approaches for techniques execution

We require these four variables in wrestling to conduct techniques, actions, and reactions, and the magnitude and smallness of such variables affect the consequence of our action or reaction. Each of these elements can impact our overall efficiency, and failing to do this will lead to the loss of scores.

Example

If we intend to accomplish a technique and are conscious of the necessity and importance of quantities and their usage but lack the essential components and factors to do so, our implementation technique will undoubtedly be inadequate, and the outcome will be less than satisfactory.

For instance, we wish to capture the opponent's single leg; however, we experience difficulty with physical strength and lack the power and physical fitness necessary to perform this technique. In this circumstance, our executed technique is rendered ineffective, and we may even lose points as a result. Our executed technique will not be produced again in the event that we have adequate physical preparation to execute the single leg technique, but we lack the requisite spirit, self-confidence, and bravery, or if it is performed, it will be insufficient and unproductive. Additionally, it will take the form of a show.

However, we may possess both of these criteria – i.e., we may be physically fit and in a positive mood when attacking the opponent's foot; however, we may lack the necessary knowledge to successfully approach the opponent's foot. The opponent's scoring and ground position techniques are unknown to us; therefore, we may possess all three of these advantages and can take benefit of them as well. These four variables can have a significant impact on our assault and put our executed technique in jeopardy.

Important note:

These four variables are inextricably linked to our opponent. The greater number of these four components, the greater our chance of achievement in both assault and defensive state. The converse is also true; the fewer of these four factors, the lower our adversary's effectiveness probability. It all relies on the two fighters and which one possesses so many of these criteria.

A self-asked query that may provide the answer to many of our outstanding questions

Why can't wrestlers execute their chosen technique on everybody, notwithstanding the fact that they understand and know all of the techniques? Why do they become unbalanced during the technique and are unable to accomplish the necessary technique?

As previously said, implementing a technique entails a number of factors. They consist of a sound and suitable technical circle, the essential physical preparation to execute the technique, the spirit and fortitude to conduct the intended technique, and the use of accurate and reasonable techniques to accomplish the required tactic. Both in defense and attack, these four components are essential to the successful execution of a technique. Each of these criteria will possess its impacts if they are not implemented. It relies on your opponent and his capability. The less advantage your opponent gains from these factors, the greater your chances of victory, and vice versa

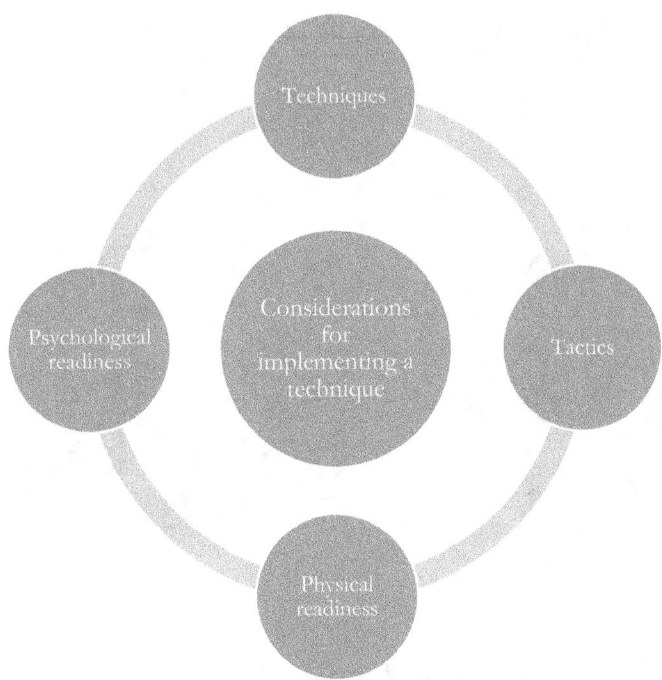

Note:
These four components are strongly linked to vector quantities, and their magnitude has a direct effect on them.

Example

Even though you're expected to have a decent approach to running a technique, you're having problems figuring out how to use quantities and prioritize them. Suppose you are unfamiliar with how to operate a technique. In that case, you must initially determine whether to use velocity or power, or you may be unsure which quantity to begin with. This failure to employ quantities results in an inadequate execution of technique. You understand how to prioritize the usage of quantities; however, you are unfamiliar with a wide range of tactics, and as a consequence, you will continue to underperform. This is due to both being inextricably linked, as are the other three factors. You have the will and bravery to conduct a technique. However, you are unsure where to begin or how to employ which quantity.

Balance and stability

What is the definition of balance?

Wrestlers must possess and comprehend the concept of balance, which is one of the most fundamental aspects of wrestling. Balance refers to the ability to maintain the body's center of mass within its base of support or to maintain the body in a variety of displacement postures voluntarily. Additionally, it is a condition in which an athlete has the capacity to maintain his position's stability.

Balance-related factors

Balance-related factors include the following:

1. Position and orientation of the center of mass axis concerning the base of support

2. Body weight; the bigger the weight, the more balanced the body.

3. The distance between the center of mass and the base of support.

What is the base of support?

Base of support refers to the space inhabited by an object in balance or, in other terms, the regions within which a person's center of mass can displace without dropping. For instance, while standing and displacing on your feet, the earth is the surface you rely on, and when lying down, the earth provides the maximum level of support for your body weight.

What is the center of mass?

A given point is considered to be such that the body can readily displace in the intended orientation surrounding it. Additionally, it is a spot on the body where the weight is uniformly dispersed to varying extents surrounding that.

Another definition of the term "center of mass" is as follows:

The center of mass is a hypothetical place where the body's weight is uniformly dispersed. The center of mass in the human body is near the umbilicus when standing and in complete balancing, and the lower the center, the stronger the balance, and the greater the center, the lesser the balance. Depending on the displacement of joints and muscular mass, the position of the body's center of

mass can shift a great deal

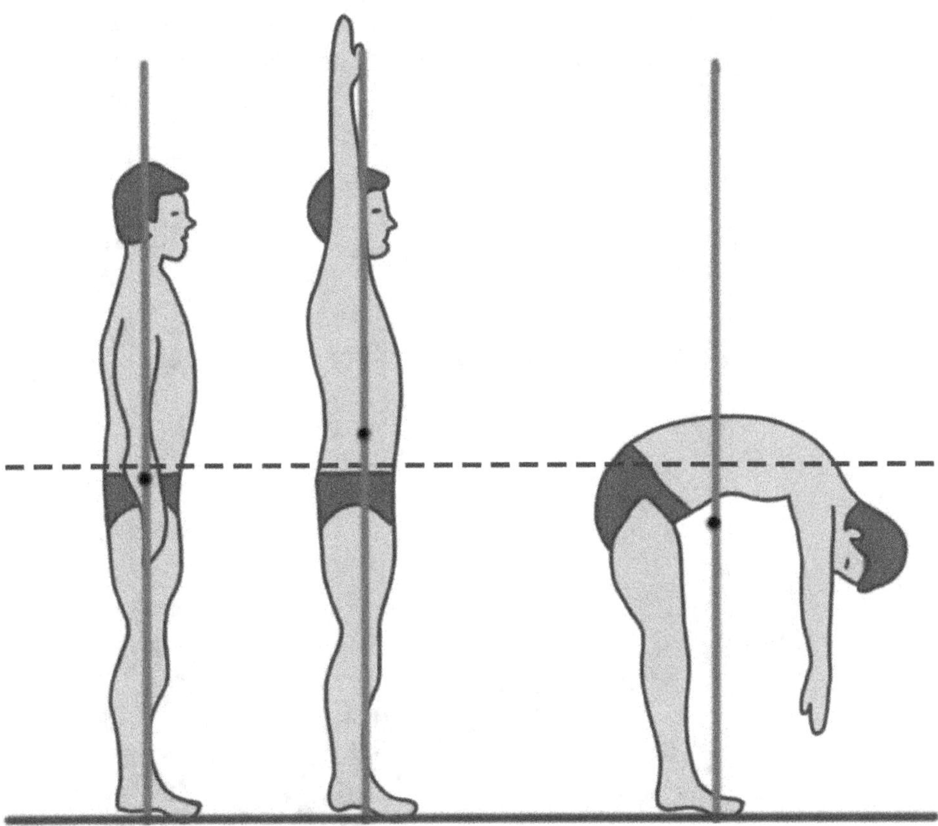

What exactly is a lever?

Levers include fundamental machines used in physics to simplify functions, including carrying heavy objects. By utilizing levers, we may enhance both force and velocity by displacing greater weights using minimal force.

Levers are classified into two types:

1- External levers that humans utilize on a daily basis, like a rod that allows us to displace an object that is heavier than us, or hand pliers, scissors, or a fork. Each of these acts as a lever, so simplifying our operation.

2. The anatomical levers present in the bodies of all humans; practically every long bone in the serves the function of a lever in our bodies, allowing us to displace.

Levers are composed of the following components:

1. Base of support

2. Force of resistance

3. The driving force

1. The base of support refers to the point on which the lever is positioned.

2. The driving force may be identical to the force applied by our hands, or it may be an external force.

3. A resistant force might take the form of a thing or an individual.

Both the driving and resistant forces have arm extensions that enable us to exert greater force or accelerate more quickly. It is possible to have more force relying on the relative positions of the resistant force and its driving force. If indeed, the length of the driving force arm is higher than that of the resistant force, we will apply more force. Additionally, assuming the length of the resisting force's arm is bigger than the driving force's arm, we will possess higher velocity.

Types of levers

Three types of levers exist:

1. First type:

The base of support is situated between the driving force and the resistant force, like the swing, in this sort of lever. Essentially, this form of lever provides balanced displacements. The velocity enhances whenever the base of support is adjacent to the driving force, and the force enhances whenever the base of support is adjacent to the resistant force

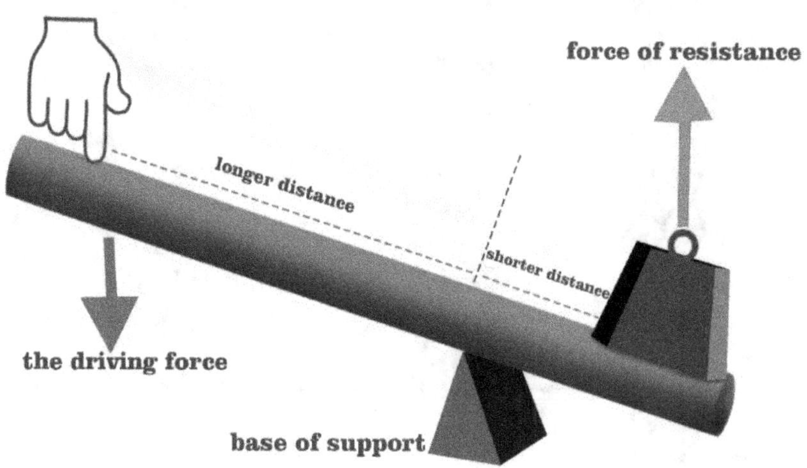

2. Second type:

The resistant force is situated between the base of support and the driving force in this sort of lever. Although this type of lever is uncommon in human anatomy and is ineffective, it is critical in conversations about executing techniques and serves a substantial function during the performance. In the following sections, we will discuss them and obtain a better understanding of their operation

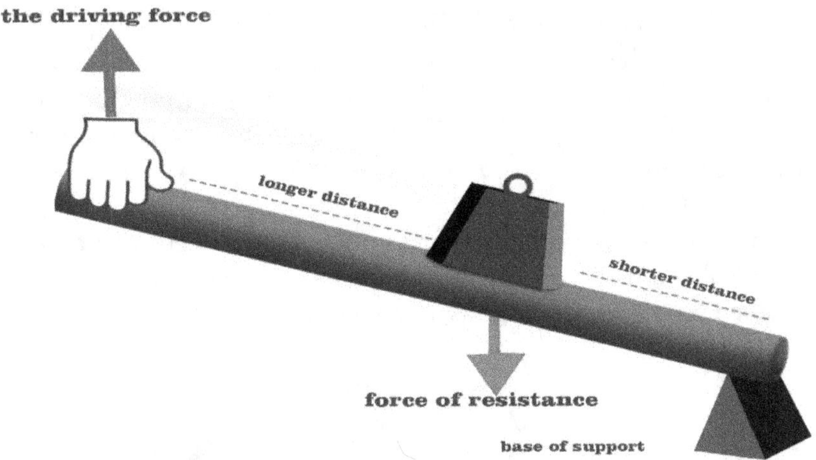

3. Third type:

The driving force is located between the base of the support and the resistant force in this sort of lever. This form of the lever is the most commonly encountered in the anatomy of the human body, and it is the lever that individuals employ the most frequently

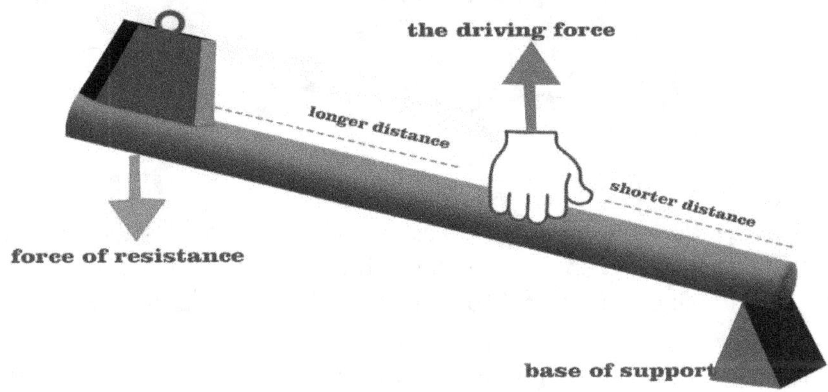

When we talk about techniques, we spend the majority of our time discussing levers of the second type, which are critical because they allow us to apply additional force.

Assume you intend to lift a lying opponent off the mat. Using the second type of lever is the only order to accomplish the function faster and with greater precision. As previously stated, there is a resistance force between the base of support and the driving force in the second type of lever. In this scenario, the resistant force is the body or opponent lying down, the base of support is your feet, and the driving force is your hands attempting to lift the opponent. As previously said, the base of support (legs) should be nearer to the resisting force (our body or opponent) in order to lift the opponent more readily, hence increasing the arm of our driving power (the force of our hands). This improves our ability to lift the body or our opponents, according to the second rule of levers. Always keep in mind that getting closer to our opponent will allow us to lift him or her more effectively from the mat. This will improve your driving force arm in any position of wrestling if you wish to lift your opponent from the mat, whether in standing, lying down, or kneeling position, and so on. As a consequence, you can lift your opponent with greater force.

Example:

While you think that you have successfully completed the single-leg technique, your opponent immediately applies a front headlock and leglever in the knee, as well as pulling his legs back. In this instance, your knees and head are bound to the mat, and you are powerless to act. The second type of lever must be used in order to get rid of the opponent's front while also earning points. That is, in order to form a larger driving arm and so apply more force, you can put your base of support (knees) closer to the resisting force or opponent.

When employing a lever, keep in mind that a higher arm length of driving force will result in a larger force applied. Additionally, you gain more velocity whenever the arm length of the resisting force is longer, which translates into increased maneuverability and displacement.

What is torque?

Torque, often known as rotational force, is a force that enables the body to rotate. Torque, in other terms, is the force that enables an object to rotate indefinitely without displacement.

Whenever an external or an internal force (the same as the muscle force) enables a section of the body to rotate, torque is generated.

These examples demonstrate the critical nature of balance. Constantly bear in mind that as the body moves away from the center of mass, its base of support diminishes, and the body appears to become unstable and unbalanced.

Example

Vector quantities are omitted from these instances.

Suppose you'd like to use the from head lock technique. To use this technique, you must initially grab your opponent's head and neck and subsequently produce torque by rotating his head and neck in one direction. After that, increasing the torque on your opponent's neck pushes his posture away from his center of mass. Thus, its base of support diminishes, and it becomes unsustainable. This inconsistency is where the technique should be run. The converse is also possible.

To overcome the from the from head lock running, you must apply a greater force in the opposite direction of the force applied by your opponent, ensuring that your body does not shift away from its center of mass. In this instance, you can sustain your base of support to avoid compromising your balance. Additionally, you should strive to maintain the body's center of mass when creating displacement and maintain a stable and balanced stance.

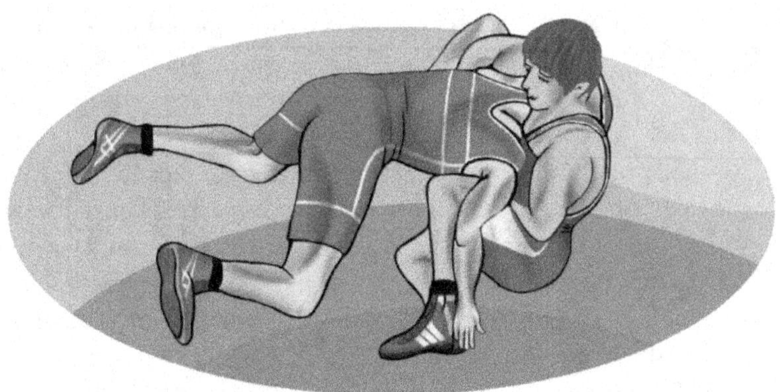

To better comprehend torque and balance, consider the following example.

This time, you are running the ankle lock. To execute this technique, you must apply a torque force or a similar rotating force to your opponent's back to dislodge his body from the center of mass and lower his base of support, which is now in his hands part. Your opponent becomes unbalanced as the base of support diminishes, allowing you to implement your technique.

Example:

Of course, I must point out that other aspects and quantities required in executing the strategies have been excluded from these examples. To help you better comprehend this issue, the statement emphasizes torque, the center of mass, the base of support, and balance.

Positioning

What does the term " positioning " imply? Almost everyone who has had some involvement with or mastery of wrestling is acquainted with this term and has heard it at least once. On the mat, coaches frequently tell pupils about positioning, and reporters frequently employ this phrase. It is frequently stressed on positioning whenever reporting on wrestling competitions, and this is a word that we are continuously hearing and are familiar with. However, what precisely is positioning, and what benefit can it provide us that we are putting so much emphasis on it? Some even regard this aspect to be a parameter in field victories.

What is the point of this positioning, which everyone recognizes as significant but which the majority of people do not get or comprehend entirely? We have undoubtedly witnessed numerous times that when the positioning command is given, the majority of wrestlers displace their hands immediately and with high intensity, attempting to strike the opponent's head and neck with tremendous force and velocity. Is the true definition of positioning that we must rapidly and violently place our hands on the opponent's head and neck to disrupt the opponent's concentration and allow us to gain points and dominate? Alternatively, it may have a different meaning that we are not informed.

While it is true that this way can expedite and intensify the work and frequently results in caution of the opponent or interrupting the opponent's balance, focus, and retreat, this does not imply positioning, but rather our touching.

So, what exactly is this true positioning?

Indeed, positioning is displacing our hands, particularly our legs, to surmount our opponent's hurdles and create a new chance for us to execute our techniques or to hinder our opponent from forming probable assaults.

Indeed, you read that correctly: the delicate and significant element of positioning is found in how we displace our legs. You may be asking how positioning correlates to our legs. However, without displacing your legs, you will be unable to perceive new circumstances, which means that it is critical that the legs function properly. Legs must be utilized to change positions and engage in what is known as positioning. The displacement of our legs on the mat, in reality, provides us with fresh chances to score points or not, as well as revealing new openings and apertures. Our positioning will be of little value if we cannot use our feet appropriately. Our opponent must also react and adjust his previous position when we switch the direction of our legs. As a result of our opponent's reaction, we will have a new opening to traverse through barriers and accomplish our technique.

We can displace our legs in all four directions, and our elevation compared to our opponent is controlled by them. We can find new situations or create possibilities for ourselves by shifting our elevation in guarding as a result of these adjustments in four directions. In order for proper positioning, we must engage our legs in conjunction with our hands when positioning. I hope you comprehend the significance of positioning and your legs and that you recognize that working your legs and displacing them around on the mat is considerably more vital than positioning.

The ability to use your legs effectively will surely increase your chances of achievement in positioning and in generating new conditions. As a result, your effectiveness rate will be increased while attacking and defending.

To illustrate the significance of legs in wrestling, consider the following:

Consider the following scenario: your coach gives a positioning order, and you stand in front of your opponent without using your legs and repeatedly move your hands on opponent's neck and head, striking forcefully and quickly. What is going to happen? You'll observe that not much happens, and you won't have much chance in practice and won't find a new opening aside from pushing the opponent back a little, confounding him, and making him imbalanced. The outcome of your positioning to obtain points from your opponent is primarily a waste of energy and increased fatigue rather than accomplishment. You will notice that the scenario transforms and that you will have fresh chances to execute the technique once you participate in your legs and displace them in various directions while increasing or decreasing the elevation of your guard relative to your opponent. In this condition, you can establish positions and implement techniques, and the quicker your hands operate, and the more you displace your legs, the more options you can present. Two critical aspects in achieving new positions are displacement velocity and power.

Laws and regulations before attacking

It is necessary to have the four components listed above in order to begin an attack. You must also understand the background and how to fight your opponent with as great intelligence and consciousness as practicable. You should not function emotionally; if you do, your attack will be dangerous, your achievement probability will be low, and you will likely lose scores. In exercise, it will take you a lot of energy and time, but your opponent will get a lot of scores. It is certain that any attack will have repercussions. Now, if it is proper and principled, it will result in points being earned; nevertheless, if it is emotional and unexpected, scores may be lost. Presently, if you don't lose scores, your time and power would be squandered, so how should you handle this condition?

How should attacks be planned?

How wrestling's attack principles are founded:

Attack commencement

1. Identifying or attempting to attack or exploit an opponent's conduct
2. Positioning
1. Interrupting the opponent's concentration or perplexing and perplexing the opponent, which is separated into two subgroups: 1. momentary, 2. intermittent (a portion of the same positioning)
2. It may involve obstructing the opponent's standpoint and so "blinding" the opponent's viewpoint.
3. The element of surprising can be utilized.

Following the selection or recognition of one of the items, the following stage is to thrust your head forward in advance of the other portions of your body to speed up and displace your legs to get closer to and therefore dominate your opponent.

4. Executing the appropriate technique while simultaneously exerting a great deal of force to demolish everything in your path and utilizing high velocity to avoid the reaction and potential reaction from your opponent (velocity in power combined with acceleration).

5. Sustaining quantities and exerting pressure to carry out interactions in an attack until it successfully gains scores. Depending on the likely reaction of your opponent, you may need to execute a technique in many quantities. The critical point is to keep putting pressure on the opponent until the desired outcome is obtained.

6. If the wrestler performs the correct approach in the commencement and follows all of the laws, he is likely to have prevented many interactions in the following stages of the match.

How to defend?

A reactive behavior, defending entails first being able to respond effectively to an attack, which is an action taken by our opponent in order to be successful. Whenever we are defending or reacting, we must apply the same four elements and emphasize the usage of quantities. When defending, you should keep the following points in mind: 1. physical fitness, 2. a positive attitude toward the opponent, 3- employing suitable and effective tactics against the opponent, and 4- employing the proper technique to counteract the opponent's attack. To begin, you must adhere to the principles to avoid giving your opponent an appropriate position, and thereafter you must possess adequate reaction power to counteract the opponent's attack with an adequate reaction. The second element to remember when defending and reacting correctly is the employment of quantities and selecting which quantities to employ in specific situations. Frequently, you must apply resistance force instantaneously upon displacement, or you must apply a greater resistance force than your opponent to gain a brief period for yourself. To get rid of your opponent's attack, you must first search for displacement or eccentric force. Throughout this period, velocity should be a key component of your work. Be mindful that when defending, it is feasible to modify the type of quantities used in response to the actions and reactions of each wrestler continuously. Within a very short period, and relying on the quantity applied by your opponent, you must determine the quantity required immediately. Positioning is a preventive arm in numerous wrestling scenarios because it prevents your opponent from forming techniques.

The relevance of vector quantities, as well as their function in forming the approach and how to deal with them, is something I hope I have demonstrated to you.

The process of technique development

To facilitate and define the route, there should always be a strategy in place that separates the main road from the devious roads and establishes the pathway. To that end, I'll show you a method of growth or development cycle in a succinct manner so that you don't get lost in the meandering route of wrestling.

Development process (technique):

There are invariably four factors to take into account when growing, and you must adhere to these four principles in order to make advancement. These four criteria are applied to all five wrestling fundamentals, and you should consistently operate in accordance with these criteria.

Wrestling is a sport in which there are four aspects that contribute to success.

1. Diagnosis, 2. Analysis, 3. Solution, 4. Practice

Technique development

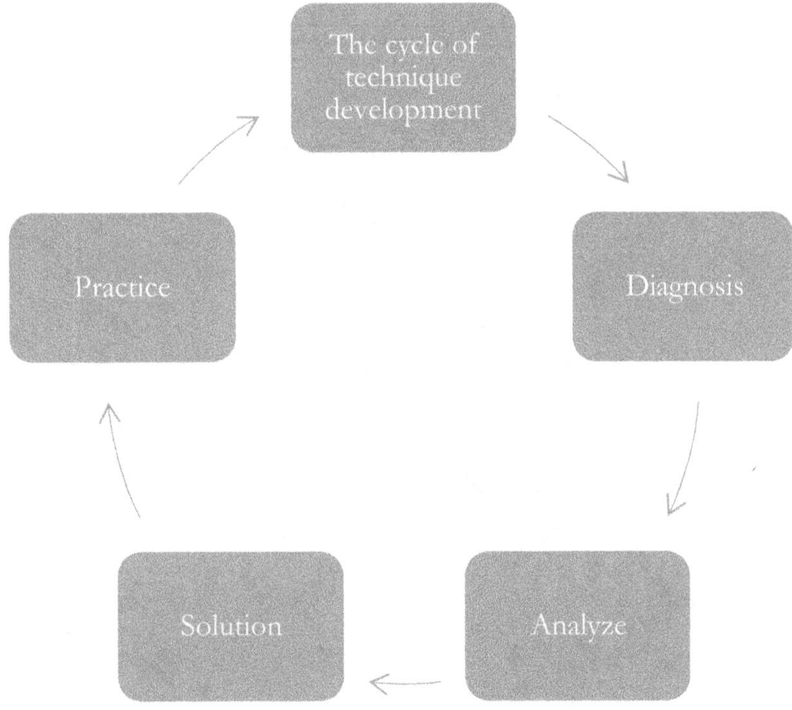

1. Diagnosis: The initial step toward growth and the most critical aspect of technique development is to identify and evaluate all technical dimensions, particularly the wrestler's capabilities and shortcomings. The primary issue in making an accurate identification is that when we are unable to produce a correct and rational identification, the outcome of our effort will almost likely be unsatisfactory.

2. Analysis: Upon recognizing and determining the athlete's technical shortcomings and capabilities, it is essential to assess and describe the athlete's shortcomings and capabilities and to look at the factors that contribute to the athlete's incapability to execute the technique, including technical, physical, mental and psychological, and tactical vulnerabilities.

The four variables indicated previously account for the majority of technical shortcomings and incapacity to implement the techniques. The individual may be unfamiliar with the techniques and their associated disciplines. Additionally, physical infirmity and a deficiency of sufficient physical fitness preclude the application of techniques. Additionally, failing to maintain sufficient spirit and motivation to carry out the techniques prohibits you from earning points. The athlete may possess the appropriate technique and physical fitness level, or he or she may lack an effective plan for performing the techniques.

3. Solution: Once you have identified the issues and assessed and classified them, you should propose a solution and employ a number of relevant approaches to resolve the issue. Solutions can be regarded and implemented in accordance with the nature of the problem.

4. Practice: The final step in improving your performance skills is to put them into practice. Thus, you may put what you've understood into practice, and you'll take a step toward success and advancement.

This is a cycle of technique progress and improvement, and it is also applicable for the other five components of wrestling, and it must continuously be the same in each area.

Chapter 2

Physical preparation

Introduction

One of the most significant aspects that a wrestler must have in order to demonstrate his ability and walk the route to success is the notion of physical fitness. As previously said, a professional wrestler requires the five fundamentals of wrestling to succeed. He will surely be one of the most successful wrestlers if he learns and applies these five concepts. These five principles are as follows:

1 .Appropriate and adequate technical circle or technique

2 .Excellent physical fitness

3 .Extreme mental strength

4 .Suitable strategy/tactical approach

5. Managing one's athletic life

This section will discuss ways to maintain physical fitness while wrestling. Physical fitness is one of the instruments that can have a significant part in an athlete's performance, and it is also a fundamental component in wrestling competitions. Physical fitness, however, is not fundamental for a wrestler and is simply one of the main foundations and instruments in wrestling. Take note that the notion of physical fitness is simply one component of a wrestler's achievement. As a result, it has been observed that some wrestlers place a high premium on physical condition and attribute their success to it. As a result, individuals frequently pursue physical fitness throughout the year, which is a misunderstanding. Physical fitness is a value that should be attained via preparation and adhering to certain standards. It is obvious that you must have a prepared body in order to demonstrate your capabilities. However, it also necessitates meticulous planning in accordance with its concepts and norms. If one wishes to be competent in obtaining physical fitness, he or she must first understand how to exercise and adhere to the fundamental principles of exercise. This is the first step in the subject of how to acquire physical fitness. Athletes must perform a range of activities to obtain their optimal physical function or fitness level. The majority of athletes engage in a range of exercises throughout the year to maintain their desired level of fitness. It is necessary for them to develop and implement a training plan to avoid becoming confused and stressed when exercising to reach their aspirations and objectives. The question now is, how should these programs appear in order to guide us in the right direction? To begin the journey toward the threshold of acceptable and desired physical fitness, one must first master the fundamental concepts and regulations of training. Therefore, you must undertake a step in this direction to ensure that the work is conducted in accordance with scientific and accurate standards.

Therefore, we must initially understand how to exercise and become familiar with the concepts and frameworks of education to gain excellent physical fitness and take the appropriate steps toward attaining maximum physical fitness.

Practice

As with our workouts, our exercises have both physical and non-physical components. The same five principles indicated above must be followed in wrestling to increase our athletic performance, which has a broad scope. (1. Technical activities 2. Tactical practices 3. Exercises for physical fitness 4. Exercises for mental fitness 5. Management training exercises). For the time being, we will concentrate on fitness training and then proceed on to other fundamentals.

Ten practical concepts

1. Diagnosis principle or training features	This principle denotes that the upcoming exercises will be relevant and specific to the same field. You must first define your plan before you begin training for a specific objective. The muscles and energy systems specific to the same field should be engaged in the exercises. First and foremost, the athlete's level must be determined. Afterward, based on the results of the examinations and physical fitness tests, he should begin training.
2. Overload concept	As the name implies, the principle of overload refers to the pressure we experience during training. But to boost an athlete's performance and prevent injury or weakness in their athletic performance, the training pressure should be increased gradually. Example: Resistance or weight training, weekly training intensity, and number of weekly training sessions
3. Adaptability principle	The adaptation principle implies that athletes will initially become weak and exhausted while performing exercises. With continued participation in this training program, the body will adapt to the exercises, and the individual will undergo changes.
4.Advancement principle	The athlete should be aware that advancement in sports performance will not occur overnight. As a result, he must initially adapt to the exercises before making progress by increasing the training load.
5. Diversity principle	The exercises should be designed and scheduled so that the individual does not become exhausted. You can, for example, change the location of training, arrange different types of training, or use various training opponents to address this shortcoming.
6. Principle of personal differences	It is important to understand that every athlete has a unique body and physiology and that this affects how they respond to various types of exercise. Accordingly, the types of exercises should be specially designed for each individual as much as possible, and a universal approach to exercising should be avoided.
7. Reversibility principle	By engaging in exercises and other physical activities, the body will grow and become more physically capable, according to the reversibility principle. However, if there is a long period between training and rest, this level of good physical performance is not enduring and will gradually deteriorate. Maintaining a state of preparation in the body is important. For instance, there shouldn't be any time off between matches.
8. Principle of persistence	According to this principle, success and the process of

	progress do not happen overnight. Instead, success requires hard work and patience. As a result, the field shouldn't be left unfilled, and one should put forth a consistent effort over a long period of time while facing challenges in order to succeed.
9. Principle of warming and cooling	It should be mentioned that the importance of warming up and cooling down the body before and after exercise should not be underestimated to prevent injuries. By warming up, we can increase and improve the blood flow to the organs and significantly lower the risk of sports-related injuries. In practice, by performing light and stretching exercises during cooling, we can decrease the amount of lactic acid in our muscles when they return to their original state and safeguard our muscles from cramping.
10. Moderation principle	As the name implies, you should not overdo and underdo in sports. If we behave in this manner, we will unavoidably fall into two groups: overtrained or undertrained. In this instance, the process will reverse and lead us away from our objective rather than moving forward and making progress.

For every sport to yield results, it must adhere to these ten criteria. Weaknesses in each of these ten criteria will have negative effects on our sport and will jeopardize our ability to continue to advance. As a result, we should constantly and strictly adhere to these ten criteria when performing our sporting activities. These are the ten most common training standards, which are well-known among athletes.

1. The diagnosis principle or training features, 2. The overload concept, 3. The adaptability principle, 4. The advancement principle, 5.The diversity principle, 6.The principle of personal distinctions, 7.The reversibility principle, 8.The principle of persistence, 9.The principle of warming and cooling, 10.The moderation principle

Physical fitness

The preparation of the muscles is only one aspect of physical fitness; the preparation of the body's systems and physiological functions must also be considered for an athlete to show his or her ability on the field. The preparation of the cardiovascular system, respiratory system, brain system, and muscle system are examples of such procedures.

Physical fitness is comprised of two components:

1. General and normal physical preparation

2. Specialized physical preparation

General physical fitness

General physical fitness corresponds to the extent to which the body has been prepared so that the wrestler conducts his or her sports exercises with ease during his or her regular and everyday practice.

Specialized physical fitness

This sort of physical preparation is purpose-specific and is intended to be utilized for a specified period of time. It is frequently anticipated prior to the commencement of the competition, and its length is controlled by the wrestler's degree of physical fitness. It necessitates meticulous and systematic planning, resulting in maximum physical fitness in the days preceding the competition. Since one must compete at best possible level of physical fitness, and because the duration of physical fitness is brief and, preferably, does not continue longer, the strength of the workout will gradually decline. Depending on the individual, this process may happen twice a year; nevertheless, it is not necessarily true that a person is best prepared by engaging in physical activity throughout the year. It must consequently be achieved by careful and fundamental planning. The time spent preparing must be coordinated with our critical competition to ensure that we are at our optimum physical fitness before our vital competition.

Suppose you want to achieve the optimal degree of physical fitness, even at a high level. In that case, you must have comprehensive and exact knowledge of your body and adhere to a sound and disciplined strategy over a certain period. Additionally, you must set aside a number of parameters to achieve the threshold of physical fitness.

We'll begin by outlining how to properly prepare your body. Afterward, we'll go over some of its more specific themes and familiarize you with the many sorts of physical fitness exams and other relevant assessments.

The average athlete should be aware that he or she will not achieve maximum physical fitness more than twice a year, which is attributable to several variables, including the type of nutrition and relaxation, kind of training, age, and inheritance, among others.

After considering this, we come to the conclusion that we should concentrate on physical fitness and avoid putting too much strain on our bodies to prepare for each competition. I believe it is incorrect to believe that to achieve success, you must continuously sweat and exercise tirelessly and put your body under a lot of tension. Furthermore, we should not expect to observe achievement just through extreme physical exercise.

If you approach this field with this mindset, you should expect your sport's life to be brief, pointless, and meaningless, with the complete reverse outcome. To strive for achievement and to put out significant effort and sweat, it is necessary to do so in a principled manner and on the basis of scientific and technological knowledge rather than on the basis of outdated and unfounded feelings and attitudes.

In order to achieve the maximum high physical ability, one of the strategies that might keep the athlete away from overtraining, standard heavy exercising, and sports problems is a reference to a large tournament as the final objective in annual programming. The remainder of the year's tournaments, which are less significant, are well attended with minimal preparation. In order to compensate for physical shortcomings, we must consider other wrestling aspects and, to a certain degree, conceal our physical deficiencies with other significant aspects of the sport of wrestling. This helps to prevent chronic muscular tiredness and damage while also saving time and energy.

One of the reasons wrestlers continue to struggle to achieve their goals despite the high level of training pressure is because they engage in unnecessary and exhaustive training, squandering their time and power, and ultimately encounter overtraining. Their motivation for success is lowered as a result, and they are unable to achieve the desired outcome. Since they believe that wrestling and success are solely dependent on physical fitness, they are uninformed that wrestling is a package in which other aspects play a role, and physical fitness is merely a component.

As a result, it is critical to understand that to accomplish this, and one must have a strategy and follow through with their science and expertise. It is necessary to dispel the illusion that one can advance and succeed with a great deal of practice and significant daily pressure. Since these incorrect workouts will not only prevent you from being successful but will also put you in danger and cause you distress. As a result, you will postpone exercise and will get several damages, which will overwhelm your wrestling and diminish your athletic period.

Before we discuss physical fitness, I would like to familiarize you with the internal tissues that play a significant and critical role in our fitness level. Afterward, we will quickly describe how they function in the body so that you may become familiarized with them, comprehend their role in body preparation, and appreciate the significance of these internal organs.

The human body is comprised of several systems and technologies, with each organ performing its function to ensure our survival. Our health will very certainly be jeopardized if a problem occurs in one of our internal organs.

However, we are not going to discuss the body's internal systems here; instead, we will concisely introduce you to a few of these systems and explain their function in preparing your body for exercise.

Internal body systems

1- Cardiovascular system:

One of the most significant and vital organs in the human body, the heart, is necessary for life to exist. Without it, the body would be unable to function. The heart is a blood-pumping tissue that transports blood and oxygen to all regions of the human body's muscles and organs, and it also serves as a source of energy for the body in general. As you are aware, our body requires energy for activities, and food provides this energy in the shape of ATP. This energy achieves the entire body by the heart; thus, to obtain the necessary preparation and accomplishment, we must prepare and strengthen the heart in the same way that we prepare and build our musculature.

2. Respiratory system

In the same way our muscles and tissues require blood and energy to function, they also require oxygen to develop the metabolic activity that allows us to do so. Without oxygen, it is impossible for us to continue living, as you already know. This oxygen in the air is absorbed by our mouths and nostrils before entering our lungs. The lungs are responsible for delivering oxygen to the cells of the body and for expelling carbon dioxide from the system. To ensure that the body obtains the oxygen it needs, the heart directs blood to the lungs, where it is oxygenated. The heart then distributes the oxygen throughout the body via the circulatory system and arteries. Because our metabolic activities depend on the oxygen in our blood, the more activity we can undertake and the longer it takes for our muscles to become fatigued directly correlates with the amount of oxygen in our blood. Therefore, we must have a robust respiratory system and train it just like any other muscle in order to prepare our bodies as much as feasible.

3. Nervous system

Throughout the body, the nervous system coordinates and supervises the functions of every organ and muscle, and it is represented in every part of the body. This system analyzes all of the data coming from the outside and the inside of the human body via the brain, and it communicates with the rest of the body using the nervous fibers. Without this system, it is inconceivable to do any action, and the body's activities will be severely interrupted. In the world of athletics, this mechanism is referred to nerve-muscle synchronization, which is something that you have likely heard of several times.

4 .Skeletal system

Our skeletal system, also known as our body skeleton, is analogous to the skeleton of a structure, which is responsible for preventing the building from collapsing. Its purpose is to preserve the body's structure and safeguard our internal organs (including the heart, lungs, and brain), and in a manner, it is also responsible for motion and velocity in our body. Our bones are one of the components that allow us to move around and be mobile. When our bones and muscles work together in unison and complement one another, we can manipulate movement and accomplish things. Consequently, we require our bones for movement and athletic participation.

5 .Muscular systems

About fifty percent of our body is comprised of the muscular or muscular systems or muscle fibers that have a significant and fascinating function in our exercise and athletic functions.

A quick description of this system should be provided so that you become conscious of this system and how it functions in exercising and comprehend the significance of this system in your wrestling. This will allow you to gain a better understanding of the muscles and their significance in the process of working out. As previously said, muscles or muscular structures comprise up to fifty percent of the human body and are responsible for locomotion. Thus, the food we consume is turned into energy and supplied to these muscles, allowing us to perform and operate via these muscles.

The human body contains three types of muscles

1. Skeletal muscles: These are the voluntary muscles accountable for protecting the bones and moving the body.

2. Heart muscles: They are components of the involuntary muscles and are accountable for pumping blood throughout the body.

3. Smooth muscles: They are accountable for the internal functions of our bodies, including the stomach and intestines, although we have no connection with this type of muscle.

However, we are primarily concerned with skeletal and voluntary muscles, their role in human flexibility and exercise, and how they influence sports motions.

Muscles characterization

The human body is composed of a great number of muscles, each of which performs a specific function. Each muscle is composed of a vast number of fibers or muscle fibers, which serve as the primary structural components of muscles. These muscle fibers provide motion for us by contracting or shrinking and extending. They are the source of movement, similar to a spring that generates motion by contracting and relaxing it. We are able to perform our activity because of the muscle's ability to contract and expand, and this process is ongoing and unending for as long as it is necessary for us to move around and be energetic.

Clearly, sportsmen are in desperate requirement of this kind of system. Due to their extensive participation in sports, individuals should be sufficiently familiar with this system. Owing to the contraction and extension of the muscles. These are the muscles that influence our strength, velocity, and durability.

It is important to note that while some of our muscles are employed for aerobic exercise, others are employed for anaerobic function. There are distinctions between these muscles based on the type of physical genetics and the sort of our activities. The distinction lies in the size and capacity, as well as their slow or rapid contraction, which is what causes some people to be quick and nimble while others have a great level of physical endurance. There is another muscle group, however, in small numbers, that are a mixture of the two preceding categories. This indicates that their muscles are both fast- and slow-twitch, which are referred to as enduring muscles.

Therefore, what is the meaning and principle behind this rapid or slow contraction?

Slow-twitch muscle fibers are muscles with a slow contraction or shortening pace. Fast-twitch muscle fibers are also muscles that can contract rapidly.

The following are the features of these two muscle groups:

Slow-twitch muscle fibers shorten later or contract later, but they have a longer duration of contraction and endurance, and they exhaust later. Because they receive more oxygen, utilize all the body's energy sources (fats, proteins, and simple and complex carbohydrates), and react to nerve signals later. They furthermore respond and react later.

The speed and duration of contractions in fast-twitch muscle fibers are increased, and the muscles' ability to generate contractile force is greatly enhanced. However, they become fatigued in a short period and consequently sooner. They receive neurological signals and react more quickly thanks to the breakdown of glucose or glycogen, which serves as their fuel.

Keep in mind that our workouts either require slow-twitch muscle fibers (aerobic exercises) or fast-twitch muscle fibers (anaerobic exercises).

In fact, there are other muscle types recognized as inexhaustible muscles that are extremely rare and only accessible to a very small number of people. They are essentially a blend of fast- and slow-contraction muscles that react favorably to both aerobic and anaerobic exercises.

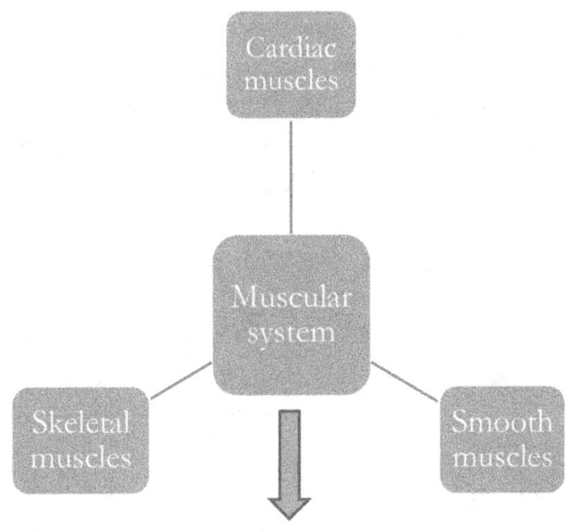

Slow-twitch muscles	It twitches more slowly, responds more slowly, tires later, and receives more oxygen. Aerobic exercise-specific muscle - fuel use from all sources (carbo-fat-protein)
Fast-twitch muscles	It twitches quicker, responds faster, fatigues faster, and receives less oxygen. The fuel utilized for glycogen breakdown or glucose is specifically designed for anaerobic workouts.
Inexhaustible muscles	This muscle model possesses both fast-twitch and fast-twitch properties.

In terms of physical fitness requirements, wrestling is one of the sports that primarily calls for endurance, speed, strength, and other characteristics. Weight training is one of the most effective ways to strengthen most of these two muscles. This can speed up and thicken our muscular fibers to gain more power, as well as strengthen and thicken our muscles through weight training. The type of weight training should be determined based on whether the muscles are fast-contraction or slow-contraction, the type of muscles, the goal, and the training program.

The significance of weight training

Why do we have to use weights?

Weight training, as everyone knows, makes muscles stronger and more voluminous. As a result, everyone strives to become stronger and more voluminous, and they often achieve this by using weights and bodybuilding equipment. To build a stronger, more voluminous physique and more stamina, wrestlers naturally follow this work and train with various weights and conventional techniques. All athletes are generally familiar with the various techniques and exercises for muscle building and strengthening that can be found in publications, books, and other media. The question, "Why do we have to weigh, and what is the goal of weight training?" is less frequently asked, but I won't say it again.

Weight training, as previously stated, helps strengthen your body and muscles. In this manner, when you lift weights and apply pressure on a set of muscle fibers in your body, the fibers are initially stimulated and then partially destroyed. The body will have to repair the torn muscles and fix the problem as a result of the pressure and partial destruction of these fibers. As a result, the body starts to repair and multiply cells in those areas, increasing the total number of cells there. This causes the muscle fibers in that area to become thicker, stronger, and larger. These cells will grow and mend more effectively and fully if you consume enough protein and get enough sleep to allow your muscles to recuperate. As a consequence, your muscles and muscle fibers will thicken, and you will become stronger.

Remember that the number of muscle fibers or the same muscle cannot be increased, but increasing their size and strength through weight training can make them stronger.

Note:

There are two distinct forms of weight training in total:

1. General weight training, which is conducted by sportsmen in bodybuilding clubs and is thought to strengthen all of the skeletal muscles.

2. Specialized weight training that concentrates on a particular target in one or more muscles and varies depending on the type of target, weight training style, and approach.

Our motivation for weight training demonstrates precisely what our muscles require and what we demand from our muscles in general (speed, strength, endurance, flexibility, etc.). Our kind of weight training changes due to individual physical variances between athletes, and each athlete physically desires his/her training plan. In general, the needs of the desired athlete should be specified. As a result, before deciding what kind of weight training is required, the body conditions must be evaluated and analyzed.

To advance in wrestling, does a person require strength training using weights, speed training using weights, flexibility, and so on?

We will surely experience weakness and failures as a result of our efforts and fail to achieve the favored outcome if we are unable to accurately identify the type of weight and its amount and provide a correct analysis of what we require.

Therefore, weight training and working with weights are vital in this context; what is our goal in training with weights? We will certainly not advance despite our best attempts if the selection of weights and the method of weight training are not based on physical analysis. We will also experience flaws and deficiencies in this condition.

Example:

You may have slow-twitch muscle fibers and not require a lot of endurance movements using weights. This implies wasting time and energy, or the opposite. To improve your athletic performance, you must first determine what you want from your muscles. Do you require speed and strengthening your fast-twitch muscle fibers? Whenever you prefer your muscles to have more endurance and tolerance, you must enhance their endurance. In general, you should always select the type and style of weight training based on your demands and avoid lifting weights indiscriminately without a justification, which will not provide excellent consequences and will divert you from your objective.

It is important to note that muscular contraction and "force generation" include two parameters:

1. The number of muscular fibers present in a muscle

2. The maximum force that a muscle fiber can generate during contraction

Therefore, it is crucial that we strengthen our muscular fibers so that they can generate more force during contraction.

To better understand muscular fibers or muscles, consider the following example:

Imagine a rubber band that is simple to pull and release. Can you simply pull like the first rubber band if you put numerous rubber bands together and then pull? Rubber bands will be more difficult to pull, as you will observe. Our muscles resemble rubber bands in many ways. If we expand the muscle fibers and their diameter, they will not stretch as readily, resulting in increased force in our muscles. Weight training, which can be highly efficient in strengthening the temporal muscles, is one of the good and acceptable solutions.

4. Energy production systems
What is ATP?

The body's muscles and cells rely on ATP as their primary energy source. ATP serves as the body's energy storage, and it is transformed into energy through food consumption.

Energy-producing systems

1 .Anaerobic without lactic acid system(phosphagen), 2 .Anaerobic or lactic acid system, 3 . Aerobic system

Athletes and wrestlers should be aware of the sources of their consumed energy.

1. Phosphagen system:

Creatine phosphate (cp) is the primary source of phosphagen. What precisely is creatine phosphate?

The body generates and stores energy by ingesting food and converting food into ATP in the bloodstream. Creatine phosphate now offers another indirect source of energy in addition to ATP, which aids in the synthesis of ATP. When energy is depleted, and ATP is broken down, it aids in the regeneration of ATP. This sort of energy is employed for actions that last less than 10 seconds, including explosive motions like a takedown. Oxygen is unnecessary, and lactic acid is not generated in creatine phosphate metabolism. Although it lasts just a short while, it is performed with the maximum intensity, and the rest interval should be three times as long as the activity. Creatine phosphate, which is stored in the body's cells, is the primary source of energy for activity. To do this, you can employ quick starts and forceful motions, and the exercises should be above average and close to their maximal power output.

2. Lactic acid or anaerobic system:

Glucose and glycogen are the primary sources of anaerobic energy. What exactly are glucose and glycogen?

Glucose is a form of sugar found in the bloodstream or the same blood sugar produced by ingesting foodstuff. Glycogen is a type of glucose stored in the muscles and liver, and during intense physical activity, the muscles utilize this sugar reserve to synthesize ATP. Fats are used by the body as fuel for lighter functions. However, when exercising intensity increases, the body's ability to metabolize fat and turn it into energy decreases. Under these situations, the body must consume glycogen to produce ATP in order to give us the necessary energy.

The incomplete combustion of oxygen in this system results in the production of lactic acid in addition to energy.

As a result of the absence of oxygen, the body secretes some lactic acid in your muscles and bloodstream when you begin using this system. On the other side, the body regulates and purifies it, so it won't be eliminated while the body continues its intense activity. In these circumstances, lactic acid accumulates in the bloodstream and muscles, and if our body's lactic acid threshold is exceeded, it turns into metabolic acid. Muscle endurance and strength will decline, and attention and alertness will also decline as a consequence.

The training lasts anywhere from 10 seconds to 3 minutes. It has a relaxation interval that is twice as long as the training limit, and it may be strengthened with 400-meter runs and up to 1000-meter runs. It is, therefore, especially effective for sports like wrestling. This condition can be achieved using an interval or intermittent technique. Training should be maximal or nearly maximal in intensity.

3. Aerobic system

Carbohydrates, lipids, and proteins that come from meals are the main energy sources of this system. Their training time ranges from 3 to 15 minutes, and their relaxation time is proportional to the level of activity. The essential energy is acquired and delivered to us by the aerobic system via food degradation against oxygen. They are utilized consistently in longer and slower exercises, including 1600 meters and endurance running. This system needs oxygen and produces no lactic acid. This system will be strengthened by increasing the training period and then the intensity of exercise. The activity-to-relaxation ratio is 1:1.

Note:

In sports, the type of training, as well as the intensity and duration of the exercise, decide which of these three energy sources should be utilized. Running and walking are examples of regular activities that activate the aerobic system. Strength and endurance activities, such as weight training, engage the anaerobic system.

The phosphagen system is activated when we need explosive movements in our activities like a takedown.

We now require to discover how these three energy-generating devices—which power our bodies and our sporting activities—provide their energy.

It is important to mention that the energy generated by these three devices originates from what sources after studying the energy production mechanisms and how to release energy in our body

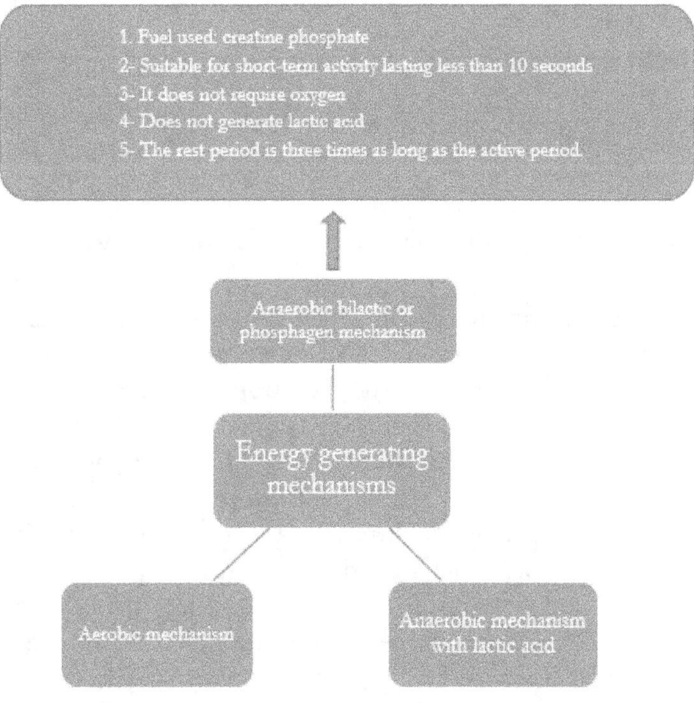

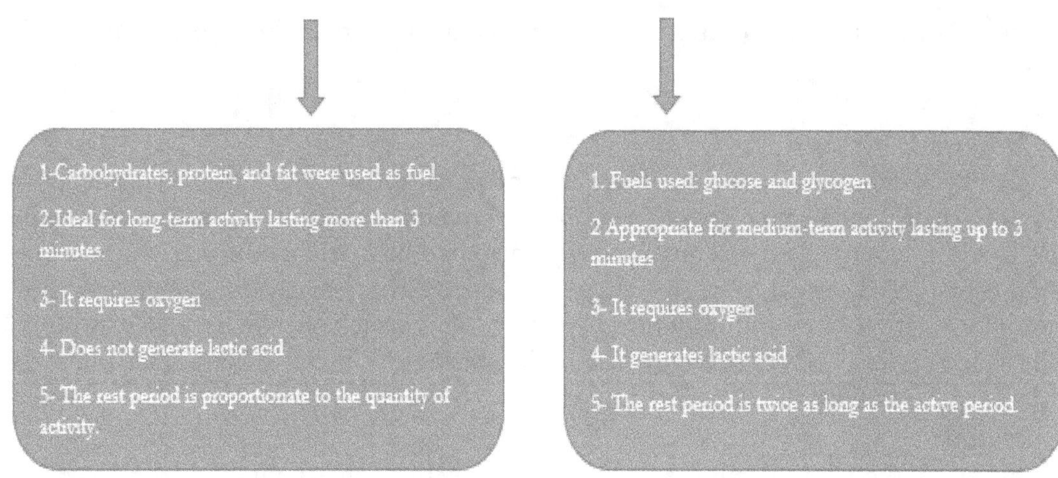

Nutrition

After being swallowed, the food is degraded in our digestive system. After interactions, it provides us with ATP and energy. Three energy-producing systems receive the energy that comes from eating food and store it according to the needs of the body and the sort of activities we engage in.

As a result, athletes and wrestlers need to be adequately informed about the food and its nutritional content.

There are six categories of nutrients in food that either help us make energy, help produce and facilitate the generation of energy, or stimulate the growth and maintenance of our bodily cells:

1 .Carbohydrates (sugars)

2 .Lipids (fats)

3 .Proteins

4 .Water

5 .Minerals

6 .Vitamins

These six molecules help in growth, maintenance, metabolism, and energy production.

Carbohydrates

 Carbohydrates, commonly known as sugars, generate the energy required by our cells. They are split into two categories: 1. Simple sugars and 2. Compound or complex sugars

Simple carbohydrates, including sucrose, sugar or fructose, fruit sugar or lactose, and milk sugar, are consumed as fuel in the body and are the fastest fuel in our body. In essence, simple sugar is anything sweet that comes from a plant source and has the capacity to be metabolized rapidly. Simple carbohydrates are small and easily absorbed by the body, immediately raising blood sugar (blood glucose) and producing energy. The fastest and most cost-effective energy source for the body, simple carbohydrates can satisfy its immediate demands.

Complex Carbohydrates are composed of long strands of simple carbohydrates that must be degraded before they can be absorbed and generated. Compared to simple carbs, they give the body energy more gradually, and because they are digested more slowly, they are less likely to convert to fats. A connection between glucose and other simple sugars, particularly glucose, occurs in simple carbohydrates like starch. These consumable carbohydrates are produced by plants, like those found in rice, cereals, wheat, barley, corn, potatoes, and other foods.

Combining glucose results in starch. It is comparable to cellulose, a form of plant carbohydrate contained in all foodstuffs. Cellulose, which is abundant in fruits and vegetables, is synthesized when glucose and other sugars are combined.

Lipids or fats:

The body requires fats, which are complex compounds composed of fatty acids and glycerin, to grow and generate energy. On the other side, it is utilized by our body to combine essential hormones. There are two types of fats: vegetable and animal. Sunflower, sesame, and olive are examples of vegetable oils and oils stored in animal fats, and milk and their derivatives are examples of animal oils. While burning more slowly and releasing energy more gradually, fats are more efficient and can produce more energy than sugars. Fat has nine calories per gram, nearly twice as much as carbohydrates and proteins. If this energy is not used up to its full potential, the body will store the excess in the form of subcutaneous fats in the abdomen and flanks to use when required.

Fats are necessary for the aerobic system to provide energy for longer-lasting activities. Long-term activity causes the release of fatty acids from the body's fat stores, which produces energy.

Proteins

One of the components of our body cells, proteins, are primarily employed for the development and repair of tissues and the synthesis of enzymes, hormones, and other chemical compounds in the body, including bones, muscles, cartilage, skin, etc. They also serve as a source of energy for us. Foods like red and white meat, egg whites, legumes, soy, etc., are all rich sources.

Proteins will not be consumed if the body receives sufficient carbohydrates and fats. The majority of our protein consumption is utilized to develop and repair our cells, and if we consume more than our body requires, it degrades proteins and stores their molecules as fat.

Protein consumption improves our athletic performance. Our muscles are both slowed down and strengthened by protein. Its overconsumption lowers muscle strength and mostly aids in energy production during aerobic exercise.

Water

Although water does not generate energy in our bodies, it serves an essential vital role in our cells as a metabolism facilitator and stimulant. Dehydration leads to hydration and dehydration during activity. Less blood reaches the body's organs to support activity because of the body's lack of water, which also decreases blood pressure and blood volume. The body finds it difficult to absorb the nutrients required by its cells and excrete wastes under these circumstances. As a result, the body temperature rises, resulting in muscle weakness and premature exhaustion.

Minerals

Minerals are not responsible for the production of energy within the body, like water, but they play a role in the production and regeneration of energy within the body. Adequate amounts of minerals are required for appropriate physical activity and metabolism.

Our metabolism requires minerals, including calcium, magnesium, sodium, phosphorus, chlorine, potassium, iodine, and iron, among others.

Example

The body's stress is reduced by calcium. Energy generation and nutrition metabolism both require magnesium. The body's energy is controlled by phosphorus, which also facilitates exercise. Sodium facilitates the transmission of nerve signals throughout the body.

Vitamins

Like water and minerals, vitamins do not contribute to the body's production of energy, but they are crucial to metabolism. Vitamins are necessary because they prevent tissue damage during intense activity and play an antioxidant role in the body.

Relaxation and sleep

One of the most crucial practices athletes should follow is getting enough sleep and relaxation. They should be as concerned about their sleep and relaxation as their workouts and sports activities. Sleep and relaxation are vital because they help our body recover. However, sleep and relaxation are beneficial since it promotes muscle growth and cell regeneration in our bodies. Because synthesis occurs during sleep, and proteins synthesized before bedtime are ingested during sleep. During sleep, growth hormones are generated and cause muscular growth or cell regeneration. Because of this, relaxation and sleep are equivalent to exercise and sports.

Each person should get 8 to 10 hours of sleep and relaxation every day, with sleep quality being considerably more essential than sleep duration. The brain must follow five stages of sleep:

1. The initial stage of sleep is the same snooze or the stage of sleep and waking that lasts a short period and accounts for 5 to 20% of our sleep duration.

2. The second stage of sleep is the basic stage of our sleep, accounting for 45 to 60% of our total sleep time.

3. The delta stage, which comprises stages 3 and 4, accounts for around 40% of our sleep and is one of the most profound stages of sleep. Our brain and body relax at this stage.

4. The body starts to operate and constitutes the active portion of our sleep in this stage of sleep, termed REM, and our heart rate and respiration increase faster, contributing to roughly 20 to 25 percent of our sleep.

To be able to follow our sports activities during the day, athletes need to sleep for about 520 minutes per night because each phase of our sleep during a nighttime sleep cycle lasts about 100 minutes.

In most cases, a good night's sleep requires a lot of effort, but getting a good night's sleep is much more essential. We become interested in sleep as a result of our mental activity and mental disputes during the day. A few elements must be considered in order to improve our sleep quality. One should not oversleep, as doing so may alter the body's biological clock, so impairing our athletic performance and making it more difficult to sleep or disrupting our sleep schedule. For instance, if our waking hours alter from 7 to 10 a.m., our bodies may still be sleepy during the competition, and we may not be able to execute properly on mattresses.

Anything that can improve your sleep quality and assist you in relaxing before bedtime should be conducted.

Before going to bed, you should stay away from alcoholic beverages, caffeine-containing foods, and other activities that will disrupt your sleep. In contrast, anything that aids in falling asleep should be appreciated. Preparing a comfortable sleeping environment, for example, or consuming meals, can improve your sleeping.

In accordance with the preceding, you are familiar with a variety of internal and external body systems that have an essential role in obtaining your favored level of physical fitness. Additionally, you have learned about the body's energy sources and processes, as well as the significance of sleep and its crucial roles in the body. Recalling the preparation-related criteria is now necessary.

A few points should be highlighted before discussing the parameters and assessments that contribute to physical fitness. Due to the importance of physical fitness to a person's or wrestler's success, it is essential to understand how to attain optimal physical fitness. This is one of the most crucial and fundamental weapons in wrestling and will help to some extent, ensure the wrestler's achievement. As a result, achieving it requires patience and perseverance as well as meticulous and consistent planning. Simply said, you must understand what you demand from your body and when you require it. Time, meticulous planning, and principles that should receive special attention are the most crucial criteria for acquiring physical fitness. It's time to make a meticulous strategy to achieve the desired physical fitness limit after completing physical fitness exams and parameters, learning about the body's strengths and limitations, and determining the level of physical fitness.

To make a plan, you must first understand the wrestler's specific physical features. At first, we may learn a lot about the wrestler's body and get a basic idea of how they are performing by, for instance, acquiring information on blood tests, body composition, age, weight class, or the state of the muscles, such as whether they are contracting quickly or slowly. Additionally, this information provides an overview of the individual's condition.

Parameters of physical fitness

These parameters are muscular strength, muscular endurance, speed, agility, physical flexibility, a reaction in a thousandth of a second, aerobic power, anaerobic power

Note:

It should be noted that owing to the scope of this subject and the complexity of each person's body and physical activities, it is impossible to fully interpret these problems and cover all of their facets in terms of physical fitness and how to attain this state. Absolutely no place will be left for further content. Since if we wanted to fully express these issues, perhaps tens of volumes of books or hundreds of different types of papers would need to be published, each of which would require extensive discussion. Therefore, to give you a clear understanding of the contents of physical fitness, we must exclude their full explanation to make space for other wrestling components. We will primarily attempt to explain a variety of fitness and physical metrics, as well as the types of assessments and how to obtain them. Even more, variables can be added to these tests. The purpose of this section is to demonstrate the significance of planning and time management in the physical fitness cycle and to familiarize you with this type of assessment and its diagrams. When you get to this level of high and optimum physical fitness at the right moment, you will reap the benefits of getting there. This is due to the fact that the human body cannot achieve its maximum physical function numerous times throughout the year, and each person's peak physical performance has a time constraint. In planning, time and management are crucial for this reason. We will first describe and categorize these parameters before tabulating the results of each assessment. We rank them from 20% to 100% based on how long it takes to achieve the preparation level. The results are subsequently recorded in each test stage, a step average of all the fitness criteria is calculated, and a point-by-point plot is drawn to show how we perform over time. This gives us the knowledge needed to know if we are making progress or not, as well as the ability to recognize our physical imperfections and areas of strength, allowing us to correct any deficiencies in some parameters. All aspects of a wrestler's physical condition must be known. We can determine a person's level of physical fitness based on the outcomes of these examinations. The type of wrestling in the competition is selected based on the outcome. We will learn from this investigation how to establish our style of wrestling and develop a general understanding of our body.

Note:

Our degree of physical fitness cannot be determined by these tests and the results, and the magnitude of the results cannot serve as a trustworthy indicator of our level of fitness. Because a person's level of preparation might vary depending on their gender, age, weight class, and other factors. However, there is no reputable source that we can cite unequivocally. However, these exams and tests might provide us with comprehension and information regarding our success or lack of progress in our physical fitness time. In this respect, several instruments and gadgets have been developed in the field of sports to supply us with these parameters more precisely and reliably. Obviously, many investigations have been conducted on these tests, and findings have also been collected and accessible as measures of physical fitness. However, these findings do not provide a convincing justification for this assumption. However, they can be viewed as assistance and guidance, speeding up the process of our physical fitness and relieving us of much perplexity.

1. Muscular strength

It is the capacity of one or more muscles to exert the necessary power in an endeavor to overcome the force of resistance. Or, to put it another way, it is referred to as the maximum force exerted on an object at one time.

What factors influence muscular strength?

They are exercise and training type, genetics and heredity, type of nutrition, gender, age, etc.

Muscular strength tests

Tests	Dead lift	Claw power	Chest press	Squat
20%				
40%				
60%				
80%				
100%				

2. Muscular endurance

Muscular endurance refers to the capability of one or more muscles to maintain strength for a longer amount of time or to maintain strength in the muscle for a longer period.

What factors influence muscular endurance?

They are exercise type, genetics, heredity, age, gender, geographical location, and type of nutrition

Muscular endurance test

Muscular endurance test	Barfix	Sit-ups	Swedish swimming
20%			

40%			
60%			
80%			
100%			

What exactly is velocity?

Speed is defined as moving the entire body in the shortest amount of time.

What factors influence speed:

They are inheritance, gender, age, body composition, muscular length, and strength

Velocity test

Velocity test	36-meter run
20%	
40%	
60%	
80%	
100%	

What exactly is agility?

Agility is the ability to shift directions quickly while still retaining balance.

What variables influence agility?

They are age, gender, body composition, muscle type, etc.

How to get to the limit of agility:

This type of examination can be passed by executing agility activities like an agility ladder, working with obstacles, etc.

Agility test

Agility test	9×4-meter run
20%	
40%	
60%	
80%	
100%	

A thousandth-of-a-second reaction

This reaction is defined as responding rapidly to any action in the shortest time.

The reaction is influenced by the following factors:

Age, gender, body composition, IQ, and nutrition

Reaction test

Reaction test	Holding a ruler with fingers
20%	
40%	
60%	

80%	
100%	

What exactly is physical flexibility?

The dynamic and static range of motion of the muscles around the joints is referred to as physical flexibility.

1. Dynamic: dynamic extending is the application of movement or force to pull a muscle.

2. Static: holding the muscle in the same position while stretching it as much as feasible.

What variables influence physical flexibility?

They are bones and muscle composition, body fat mass, skin, tendons, age, gender

Flexibility test

Flexibility test	Torso or waist flexibility	Shoulders flexibility
20%		
40%		
60%		
80%		
100%		

The scaled table can be used to acquire back flexibility. Divide the length of the hand by the distance from the wrist to the floor while lying on the floor with your chest up. This will help you flex your shoulders.

What exactly is aerobic power?

Aerobic power refers to the highest quantity of oxygen that can be delivered to the muscles during exercise.

What factors influence aerobic power:

Gender, age, sport type, and geographic location

Aerobic power test

Aerobic power test	Cooper's test and assessment of cardiorespiratory endurance vo2max
20%	
40%	
60%	
80%	
100%	

To determine aerobic power, you must run for 12 minutes straight on a flat surface, at which point you must enter the run's distance into the following formula.

(44.73)% (9/504 - distance traveled)

To determine our cardiorespiratory endurance, we entered the obtained value into the Table below.

Excellent	Good	Medium	Low	Very low	Age
50-62	44-50	38-42	32-37	32	20-24

What exactly is anaerobic power?

Anaerobic power is the maximum amount of energy that muscles can produce without using oxygen.

What factors influence anaerobic power?

Gender, age, genetics and exercise type

Anaerobic power test

Anaerobic power test	30-s Wingate in hand	30-s Wingate in foot	30-s Ergo Jump
20%			
40%			
60%			
80%			
100%			

Example

To help you understand the testing process and prepare for future tests, I'll try to give you an instance and design a dot diagram in this section.

For the 57 kg youth weight class, I will illustrate the muscular endurance test by drawing a diagram from the 20 to 100% stage.

Muscular endurance test

Muscular endurance test	Barfix	Swedish swimming (1 minute)	Sit-ups (1 minute)
20%	18	57	60
40%	17	60	63
60%	20	57	57
80%	29	65	66
100%	31	69	70

Example:

You can now build a point-by-point diagram to determine the state of growth or lack of growth in each stage by summing the data in the 20-100% stage and calculating the average of each stage

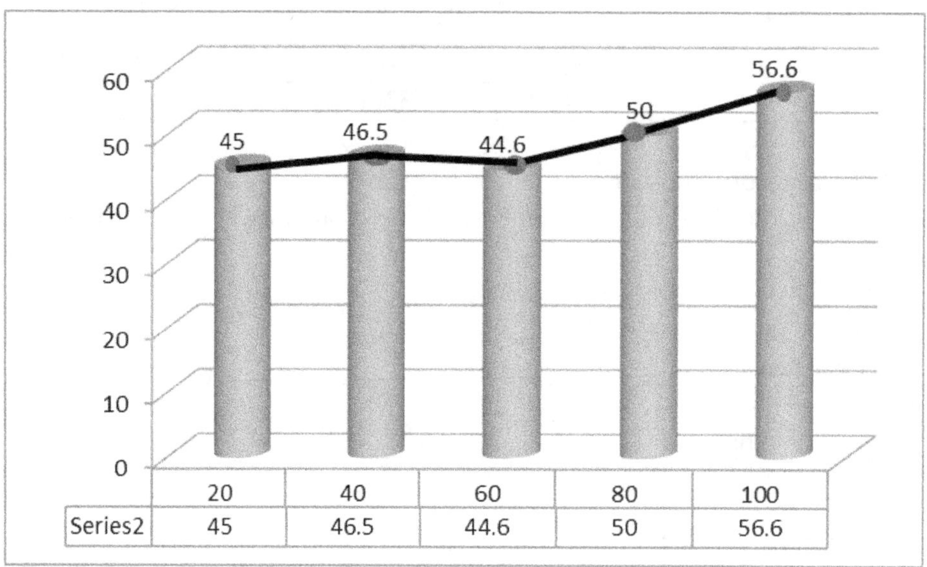

Weight loss

One of the major issues and difficulties wrestlers typically experience throughout the year is weight loss. In general, athletes perform this operation improperly, which can be exceedingly damaging and harm the wrestler's health.

Thankfully, the World Wrestling Federation just adopted the correct and rational choice to prohibit athletes from reducing too much weight. This is a very nice employment and a place that prioritizes the health of sportsmen in its decision-making. Implementing new weighing restrictions has stopped wrestlers from losing weight frequently and rapidly.

We also acknowledge and appreciate the World Wrestling Federation's choices, which are made with the athletes' well-being and fitness in mind. In the following, we agree with the wrestling union's affirmative decision, and instead of attempting to describe the procedures and principles of weight loss, we feel obligated to desist from discussing how to lose weight. Here, we exclusively discuss the risks and disadvantages of losing weight. This makes athletes conscious of the dangers of reducing weight and encourages them not to lose weight without information.

Weight loss is a two-sided coin that will be beneficial if conducted with science and understanding. Furthermore, making decisions solely on feelings and emotions will almost certainly result in several damages and losses.

Checking to discover if the individual who wants to lose weight qualifies for it is the first step in the weight-loss process. In other words, it is important to assess each person's physical capabilities in order to determine whether they can lower their body weight, if so, by how much and how quickly.

This requires first determining the athlete's body mass index (BMI). The quantity of fat tissue, muscle tissue, and bone tissue should also be examined to see if a person can reduce weight. Once the body mass index has been established, the body fat percentage of the individual must be subtracted from their muscle mass to estimate the range of weight loss or how much weight the individual is capable of losing. Only less than 5% of total body fat can be decreased. To avoid causing injury to the body, this process should be completed within a specific timeframe according to science and consciousness. Regrettably, athletes and coaches tend to ignore these recommendations and frequently believe that reducing weight rapidly and efficiently will help them achieve their objectives. Unfortunately, this type of weight loss has numerous negative repercussions on the athlete, which will be discussed in further detail below.

Unprincipled and harmful weight loss techniques

Not drinking liquids, fasting, intentional vomiting, using a long-term sauna, wearing nylon clothes, high-pressure physical exercises, using diuretic or water-absorbent medicines, and body dehydration in short-term and rapidly

Each of these approaches can, in the short and long term, result in a significant amount of psychological and even physical harm. These damages are decreased muscular strength, decreased duration of sports activity or endurance, reduced speed, cardiac failure, poor blood circulation, polycythemia, renal failure, premature aging in the long term, anorexia, decreased urination, impaired senses, dizziness, asthma, muscle cramps, dermal sensitivities, reluctance to compete, reduced consciousness, poor body growth, harmful hormonal effects, mental and psychological effects, moodiness, nervous anorexia, bulimia, etc. You might experience any of these symptoms if you try to apply the above techniques to reduce weight quickly. These approaches to weight reduction can be detrimental and harmful to your health, depending on the kind and degree of the action taken to reduce your weight. Using these techniques in such a situation will not only prevent you from winning competitions but will also expose you to a number of diseases.

Don't bother making any attempts to reduce your weight. Wrestlers' ability to lose weight quickly has been prohibited by a recent World Wrestling Federation ruling. This is an appropriate and valuable measure to preserve the health of sportsmen. To avoid hurting your health, you should decrease weight gradually.

Utilizing a long-term program, performing physical activities, reducing controlled caloric intake, and utilizing limited dehydration prior to weighing are the best ways to lose body weight in order to achieve the optimal weight for competitions. It accounts for less than 3% of total body water.

The process of gaining physical fitness

1. Diagnosis: Recognizing and realizing one's weaknesses and strengths in the area of physical fitness are the first step. This stage is critical because it includes studying the athlete's body, both in terms of internal body systems and the organs and muscles condition, including the cardiovascular system, respiratory system, nervous system, energy generation systems, and evaluating the tissues and muscles condition. All of this information can be gathered by blood testing or various sorts of physical fitness exams. These aid in determining a person's body's positive and negative aspects.

2. Analysis: Once you've identified and confirmed the existence of these problems, you should investigate and identify their causes. Afterward, details like "why a person has a deficiency in a given field and what the cause is" should be acquired.

3. Solution: Once you have recognized and analyzed the athlete's physical difficulties and faults, you must develop solutions to these difficulties. You should present a solution detailing which exercises and advice the individual should follow in order to improve his/her physical condition.

4. Exercise: In the final stage, after recognizing the problems and providing solutions, it is essential to put these solutions into action and perform them. These suggestions work together to assist us to improve and develop our physical condition.

Chapter 3

Mental preparation

Introduction

First of all, it should be made clear that due to the wide range of mental dimensions of people and the individual variances between people, we are not seeking various solutions and approaches to reach mental preparation in this section. We attempted to avoid pointing out, commanding and forbidding, and demonstrating approaches to boost spirit in this chapter. We omitted the dos and don'ts and suggestions of psychology, which are commonly accessible to everyone. We feel that a few vague pieces of advice and directions are insufficient to conquer a person's mind and bring it to a mental ideal. We have founded keeping strong morale and mental preparedness on the premise that each person first becomes conscious of his mental character, mental state, and mental framework. This is because of the wide dimensions of the mind and the mental variations of each individual. Afterward, based on the advantages and disadvantages of this field, he can decide for himself. The individual will then prepare and polish his mental approach in order to achieve the psychological standards of a professional sportsman.

We will focus on the mental framework and its importance in the subject of psychological preparation and pursue the topic more thoroughly. The objective is to be able to comprehend the mind and how it functions better and, if there is a flaw, to attempt to correct it so that we have a sound and long-lasting mental preparation. This is in contrast to the advice and prescriptions used in sports psychology, which is frequently short and ephemeral, and are more akin to a psychological analgesic than a true mind treatment.

It is important to understand something that is the foundation of all mental and spiritual conditions of an athlete and wrestler and is the cornerstone to achievement in all areas before we talk about mental preparation and how to obtain it. It consists solely of "the mind" and governance over the body.

It is important to understand the mind and how it differs from the brain before entering into this topic. This is because some people confuse the mind with the brain and do not distinguish between them. Here, we strive to first clarify the distinctions between the mind and the brain in order to dispel any confusion and improve our ability to interact with them and understand how they function.

What exactly is the mind? Is the mind identical to the brain?

No. Humans have always attempted to understand and control the mind in order to fulfill all of their inner and outside aspirations and comprehend its reality. I aim to be able to explain the mind to you in the simplest terms possible, to give you a glimpse of God's omnipotence, and to convey the idea that people are the best of all living creatures. The human body, as you are aware, is composed of a variety of parts, including the eyes, ears, tongue, hands, feet, heart, lungs, kidneys, bones, hair, brain, and mind. Additionally, our bodies contain thousands of different parts, each of which has a specific function. The mind, or the management of our body, is one of the most significant of these parts; it is something no one can feel or touch, but it is something that must be comprehended and understood in order to achieve its reality. What exactly is this mind, how can it be identified, and what are its constituents?

Our mind is divided into four sections:

Archive of memories and information, memory management, information arrangement, body management

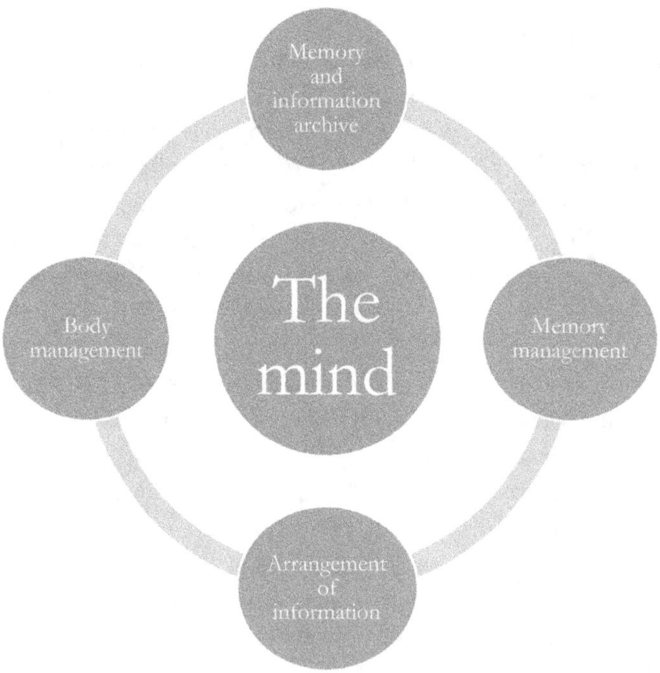

What exactly are memory and information archiving?

Memory's role, as the name implies, is to store the information that we have previously given it.

What is memory management?

This section's job is to keep track of the information we've previously provided the memory, which will be discussed later.

What is information management?

It classifies the information we've previously given it and returns it to us as needed (for instance: sadness, joy, stress, excitement, love, hate, etc.). Additionally, this arrangement gives us access to whatever we require at all times and in a variety of circumstances.

What is body management?

Body management, as the name implies, is the activity of managing the human body and providing it with everything it requires so that there is no impairment in the body's working and the body can execute its functions efficiently.

To comprehend the mind framework, consider the following example and physical analogy:

Take into account the components of a computer, including monitor, case, keyboard, power, CPU, RAM, wire, and thousands of electronic parts. The computer, similar to the human body, is composed of various sections, each of which executes its function efficiently. This enables us to use it while adhering to a program. Have you ever given the computer's most crucial component any thought? What component of the computer is necessary for following and advancing even the simplest program? The answer is yes; it is the component of the case necessary for any action to be carried out, and the absence of the case causes the other components of the computer to lose their characteristics. The power or energy supplier, motherboard, fan, wires, electronic components, ICs, programmed CPUs, and memories are only a few of the parts that make up the computer case. These aforementioned components are the parts of the computer case that enable us to monitor computer operations. The human brain is represented in the case area by the power supply, motherboard, fan, wires, and electronic components. The role of our mind is also played by programmed ICs, CPUs, and RAMs (including storing information, categorizing and filing data, working with different programs and applications, etc.). They are much smaller than our minds and help us to stick to a program. The mind functions like a computer, processing the considered programs and delivering them to us as quickly as possible. The human mind is similar to a supercomputer that can store and archive millions of pieces of data and programs and deliver them to us without making even the smallest error in a split second. We can therefore draw the conclusion that the supercomputer that God has given us functions just like a regular computer, allowing us to load whatever program we like onto it and input any data we like into its memory. We are the ones who decide if these programs and data are excellent and beneficial or erroneous data and harmful programs. Our bodies are exclusively responsible for acting on these data. The body functions similarly to a robot, acting on the basis of whatever data and program have been given to it, and there is no infringement unless fresh information and programs are installed.

Now that you have a basic understanding of the mind allow me to introduce the brain and explain how it works in the body. As previously said, the brain only serves as an operator and a source of our mind's directives. Consider the preceding instance about computer case components.

What exactly is the brain?

The brain is made up of a collection of receiving and transmitting antennas in the body that, thanks to the nerve fibers found all over our body, exclusively carry out the commands of the mind and do not participate in bodily decision-making. Furthermore, the brain serves only as an information transmitter in the body.

How do the mind function and process information?

What is the mechanism of mind-brain collaboration?

How does our mind function?

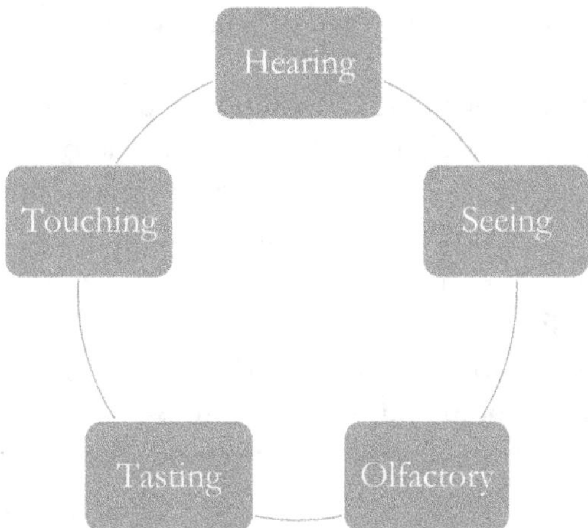

The brain first receives information from the environment through the five senses, which we will describe later (including the sense of smell, taste, sight, hearing, and touch). Subsequently, using its antennas or nerves within the body, it receives these senses and communicates them to the mind by sending a message. According to our mental filters, the mind evaluates, processes, and analyzes this message before sending it to the brain. The commands for implementation are issued by the brain in the form of a chemical reaction in the body (including adrenaline or morphine) or stressful and pleasurable hormones.

Different glands in the human body release particular hormones into the body in response to particular circumstances. It is possible that some of these hormones, which are directly influenced by the mind, acquire the executive command of hormones and so completely overwhelm our body. These hormones, including adrenaline and cortisol, which are recognized as fear and stress hormones, have a mental origin. Contrarily, certain hormones, including endorphins, serotonin, dopamine, etc., are classified as happiness and motivational hormones since they lead to enjoyment, motivation, and pleasure. These hormones possess a mental origin and get secretion commands straight from the mind.

For instance, when you see a beautiful scene with your sense of sight, the brain gets the information through the ocular nerve fibers and sends a message to the mind. Following evaluation and analysis in your mind, a command is issued based on the mental filters (since usually the mental filters identify the beautiful scene as a pleasant and good place). This command triggers the brain to secrete morphine hormone, which produces the subsequent commands in the form of a chemical reaction known as morphine. You experience pleasure and enjoyment in this situation.

In contrast, you may hear undesirable sounds with your hearing sense and ears. This information travels from the brain to the mind via the auditory nerve fibers, and a message is transmitted back to your brain after processing and analyzing in mind. In this moment, adrenaline's message has reached the brain, and as a result of a chemical reaction set off by adrenaline, the brain produces feelings of excitation, stress and unpleasantness, worry, and apprehension. All these processes occur in the human body in a fraction of a second. All the wonderful and negative events in your life could happen in the shortest amount of time. However, this is not the matter. These assertions are simply how our minds work and the appearance of the situation. Its essence must be discovered elsewhere, which is where your mental filters or mental locks are located.

So far, we've just discussed how the mind operates and how orders are implemented in the body and brain. But what is the origin of these morphine-adrenaline interactions that generate positive feelings, motivation, vibrancy, and energy or negative feelings, stress, weakness, and lack of energy in our bodies?

Only in the preceding section were we able to comprehend the mind and how it functions. However, how does our mind deliver the signal to inject morphine or adrenaline, and how does it determine when to do so? Furthermore, how does it recognize if we should be inspired and joyful right now or stressed and stressed? The solution is found in mental filters.

What exactly are mental filters?

The most important factor of our happiness or misfortune in any field is mental filters .They are essentially developed within and surrounding our lives and are based on our family and society. They can be summed up as the mental conceptions that have become engraved in our minds and serve as necessary points of reference. These filters, whether negative or positive, develop from birth with the development of our minds. Our beliefs and attitudes about an event-whether we see it as nice and positive or poor and negative-are known as mental filters. Every human has this perspective and attitude toward other people. In reality, this is the difference between people-their modes of thought and mental filters that determine who succeeds and who fails. These hormonal directives that the mind sends to the body can have a direct impact on our athletic performance, causing our bodies to fatigue and lack energy or happiness. It relies on the nature of our mental filters. The capabilities of humans are practically limitless, and they can accomplish almost everything. A person's perception of a function as achievable or unachievable is influenced by these mental filters. It is similar in wrestling and athletic competition; one wrestler will prevail, while the other will be unsuccessful. All of these arguments were presented to the point of how essential mental filters may be in wrestling and a wrestler's achievement or failure. It must be mentioned that this issue determines the inability of wrestlers to attain the necessary level of success despite extensive training and effort, as well as a high level of physical fitness. Because they lack the necessary vision filters to compete in wrestling, and their approach to achievement is flawed. They must change their mental filters and locks, as well as their false ideas and behaviors. This is the main factor in achievement in wrestling and other large fields where one individual becomes an Olympic champion while another fails.

What steps should be taken now?

Let's briefly discuss habits and their purpose in mental filters before attempting to polish the mind and mental locks so that you can gain a better understanding of the mind and its operation.

What exactly is a habit?

In actuality, a habit is an automatic brain reaction formed under specific conditions and as a consequence of increased repetition. When our acts are carried out entirely automatically, and without mental evaluation, it can be said to be a habit. If you recall, we discussed mind functions .It receives a topic via the five senses and analyzes it before issuing a command to the brain to implement in the shape of a chemical process.

A neural pathway between the brain and the nervous system is created with our mind when an action is done numerous times. This established pathway facilitates the transmission of energy from sensory nerves to motor nerves, allowing the mind to squander less energy. Since the mind, similar to the rest of the organs, requires energy, and after functioning and expanding, it becomes fatigued. This is the explanation why certain body organs strive to cease squandering energy on actions that they have already performed numerous times and instead perform what we refer to as a habit.

Habits are formed so that our minds use less energy and become fatigued later. For this reason, the mind initially analyzes and evaluates a work and a function; nevertheless, with repetition and consolidation, it does that action automatically, unconsciously, and without further analysis.

According to studies, 45% of our daily actions are habitual, allowing the mind to expend less energy. These mental habits will have both beneficial and harmful outcomes. It all depends on whether our habit is pleasant and helpful or bad and erroneous. This explains why habits are essential and impact our sporting lives.

There are three types of habits:

1. Movement habits

2. Mental habits

3. Personality habits

Our physical and muscular activities are connected to our movement habits, which can impact how well we perform in sporting events. If an athlete repeats a mistaken action multiple times, it will become a habit, and he will undoubtedly incur failures. Similarly, mental habits can have an impact on an athlete's mentality and inflict psychological damage. They are incorrect mental filters that have ingrained themselves in the person's mind and have now developed into habits. Our personality traits, including our willingness to assist others, our attention to detail, our regular schedule, etc., are all examples of personality habits.

Mental filters influence how our minds create habits. If we have effective and appropriate filters for a work, then after enough practice, that work will undoubtedly turn into a healthy and beneficial habit. If we do not have the necessary and comprehensive awareness and information to perform a function and instead employ unsuitable and inadequate filters, it will undoubtedly become a wrong and erroneous habit that will mislead us from the journey until we obtain a proper comprehension and remove our negative habit. Due to the fact that once a habit is accepted by our mind, regardless of whether it is a good or bad one, it is no longer analyzed and is just followed. So, it is critical that we concentrate on our mental filters to establish healthy and appropriate habits for us in a profession.

An example regarding movement habits

Consider the scenario when you practice a technique poorly while wrestling, and after doing so repeatedly, the erroneous approach becomes a procedure or a habit. As a consequence, this incorrect approach will be recorded in your memory, and mental archive and your mind will unavoidably show the same erroneous action when required, and you will undoubtedly suffer from flaws and deficiencies.

How may these erroneous mental filters and locks be corrected?

There are two approaches to address this weakness and many other issues: 1. By gaining "awareness" and proper information, or by using various means to receive helpful information, such as reading or seeking advice from others, or by hiring a professional trainer or an expert advisor, etc. Additionally, in general, any method that provides important knowledge will also be helpful. 2. By getting experience. Of course, this approach will be expensive, and you will have to pay the value, and it may take a long time to comprehend and achieve it, as well as rectify a misunderstanding.

Thus, the mind, like a computer upgrading, can be developed and improved so that it leads to learning by using the two following methods:

1. By gaining information and awareness and trying to understand a subject from all aspects

2. Challenging yourself and gaining experience in learning

Both approaches lead to the same conclusion. You can take the first approach to get to your destination faster and with less damage, or you can take the second approach to get there later and with more difficulties. "Authority" is yours, as it was given to us by God.

The only difference between these two approaches is time, which can be quite crucial and be a type of beginning point for one person's achievement relative to another. Because as time passes, the human body grows increasingly frail. This is contradictory to the nature of the mind, which matures and grows stronger with the passage of time and the acquisition of experience and knowledge. The mind and the body are always at odds with one another, and no person ever experiences having both on their side and moving in the same direction-unless we are blessed with the ability to use both at once. This stage of life is known as the youth and the green area of life since it is at this time that we have the vitality of youth and the circumstances needed to both receive and learn new things as well as improve our minds. These requirements can encompass getting an excellent and experienced consultant, having an informed and knowledgeable relative, or living in an intellectually normal community, including having well-meaning friends and companions, studying and expanding our circle of information, or anything else to aid our mental development and dynamism.

Due to the accumulation of knowledge or experience in various fields, people's minds frequently change during their lifetimes, and this will continue till the end of our lifetimes. You've probably heard the popular and delicious example and a proverb, "It necessitates a lot of travel to cooking crude things." What does this proverb mean? According to this proverb, a person will discover new things, learn useful lessons, and have worthwhile experiences on numerous journeys. He will also learn a great deal of awareness and information, and his point of view toward his environment will become more complete, and he will be able to examine difficulties more thoroughly and accurately. Consequently, he will make a wiser choice, which will lead to his achievement.

Example:

A competent wrestler seeks a goal for his achievement and has adequate and accurate information about it, as well as focusing solely on the goal and ignoring any other variables. In this condition, he either remains impervious to the bad thoughts that surround him, or he controls these thoughts, keeping them in his control, and its result is success. But another wrestler might not have the necessary information and expertise, or maybe he needs to go through an experience first; then, once he's done that and unlocked his mental locks, he'll be able to be sure of what he needs to do to be victorious. In other words, these grapplers are cautious because of a lack of awareness, and they won't proceed until they are convinced about something and attain a belief. These wrestlers need more time to free up their minds before a big competition. This implies that they should get experience to have a good attitude toward a large competition to be victorious and win a large competition. This necessitates a significant investment of both energy and time.

What exactly is belief?

Beliefs are our mental views of an event that notify whether we are capable of doing anything. Beliefs, which are acquired through consciousness and experience, are essentially the mental filters that give us the bravery to undertake something.

When we believe we have expertise about a particular topic, we usually reach a point of belief and assurance. This expertise and feeling of dominance are contingent upon our level of understanding and awareness of a subject. Additionally, a lack of knowledge about a subject is the primary cause of one's self-belief or lack thereof. This has the potential to either bolster our confidence and encourage us to take action, or it can weaken our motivation and cause us to feel afraid.

A belief and a certainty are the results of our collective accumulation of information, knowledge, and experiences. Now, if all of this background knowledge and experience is accurate and comprehensive, then a favorable impression can be drawn. We will have erroneous beliefs and inaccurate perceptions if our knowledge and experiences are insufficient and incomplete. All of these factors will eventually shape our positive and negative beliefs.

What exactly is fear?

Fear is a negative emotion that is originated from our minds and thoughts as a result of our mental filters and paucity of understanding about an occurrence. This condition is a chemical reaction of adrenaline, which commonly manifests as cortisol hormone, or the anxiety and stress hormone, as previously mentioned concerning how the mind functions.

A person will not feel terrified as long as he is unaware of an event. Since the mind is unaware of the situation and does not have any relevant stored information for citation, it will not react spontaneously. Fear, worry, and negative feelings develop when we have incorrect, insufficient information and experiences regarding a function or situation. This is the reason why the mind generates a chemical reaction based on the memorized information. The body will now direct the release of morphine and endorphin, which is a pleasurable and joyful experience, assuming the information is accurate and adequate. The mind will also order the release of cortisol, which causes us to sense excitement, fear, and anxiety if the knowledge and experiences provided are lacking or unpleasant. Its bodily manifestations include dry mouth, muscle weakness, tachycardia, difficulty breathing, and frequent urination.

Now, we require to continuously add to our knowledge or put ourselves in novel and difficult situations if we want to be able to have good beliefs or get rid of worry and fear. Additionally, we must experience a subject in order to have a confident, brave, and perfect mind. So, if you consider yourself a courageous and risk-taking individual, you should strive to experiment and enhance your knowledge. To succeed and avoid the difficulties and hazards of experiencing, even if you consider yourself to be careful and low-risk, you should expand your knowledge and awareness. Although combining these two factors, i.e., acquiring information and experience, is the ideal option and the best approach to advance and succeed.

What exactly is Mind control?

Mastery of thoughts or emotions is described as mind control. We should now consider a solution and take control of these filters that have accompanied us since childhood after acquaintance and learning about their significance. Furthermore, if required, we should change them, eliminate the unnecessary components, and use them in a constructive manner as much as possible in order to attain our goals. This entails mind control in order to fulfill objectives. It should also be noted that this mindset and style of thinking did not just appear overnight for us, and you wish to solve it immediately. This problem, like the body, has to be cared for and trained over time. You should first recognize the incorrect information that floats through your mind, subsequently, attempt to correct them, and develop a new perception of yourself.

Example about wrestling:

While competing against a top wrestler, you may have entered the ring with the wrong filters and beliefs. It is likely that based on previous knowledge of that person or your five senses, you have formed the notion that the opponent is stronger and you are unable to demonstrate your talents. You have unavoidably stimulated the release of cortisol hormone or fear in your body in this situation (and your mind has secreted adrenaline hormone in your body). In this circumstance, you can plainly observe that your muscles are sluggish and negligent, worry and anxiety encircle your entire self. You can obviously see that you played extremely poorly, were unable to demonstrate your potential, and lost the match. On the opposite, you have released the morphine and caused freshness and incentive by having strong self-belief and confidence in your talents, according to your worldview and way of thinking, and by providing the correct filters to your mind. In this situation, you vastly outcompete the opposition and win as a consequence, and you can control your thoughts and change the result in your favor. In this instance, you should be mentally prepared.

Controlling one's inner sensations and emotions, correcting them, and raising one's mental level in the direction of achievement is what mental preparation entails. Through your five senses, these emotions and thoughts are always accessible in your mind, and you must continually regulate and strengthen them to achieve success.

What exactly is psychic or mental energy?

We all know that that the energy required by the human body is derived from food or blood ATP and that humans are able to move and continue their activities using this source of energy. On the other hand, we would want like to familiarize you with a different kind of little-known energy. It is life energy or mental energy that is available in all humans. It has a psychological origin that we have all employed numerous times but are unfamiliar with and do not know about this energy. There is vast energy within and behind human minds that is significantly more powerful than the natural energy obtained from ingesting food. It is possible to understand the nature of this energy using a few examples.

Example:

Assume you have worked hard for a long time and are fatigued, and you return home and find yourself resting in a corner, unable to get up. You hear a loud noise at the same time, and you quickly react by running away. This question arises, as a few moments ago, you were unable to rise from the ground, but you reacted immediately when you heard this sound. When this happens, you are so shocked that you entirely forget about your previous circumstance and act without thinking. This is the hidden energy that can be utilized in different conditions. Your five senses are the primary source of this energy, but it has a mental and spiritual origin and will aid you in necessary situations. You respond right away using your mental filters, but you have no idea from where or how this enormous force is originating. The source of this immense energy is in your mind and psyche, which moves all at once and derives from your surroundings or within your mind based on your five senses or your perception and manner of reasoning about an incident.

This type of energy is really beneficial when trying to exercise, and it can be extremely effective if you can comprehend and manage it.

Consider a scenario in which you have worked out vigorously, your body has become lactic, lactic acid has covered your entire body, and you are no longer able to workout. In this circumstance, you unexpectedly become thrilled when you view a scene (sense of vision), and you ignore your starting position in a state of weariness and begin doing hard and more strenuous physical activity with tremendous intensity. How you immediately perform actions that you were unable to do when your body was in an acidic state while you could not get up off the ground just seconds before? You can exert more effort during your sporting activities because of this energy hidden in your mind and is instantly mobilized based on the situation and your mental evaluation. Suppose we can acknowledge this immense God-given energy, become informed of its powers, and take hold of this energy. In this case, we can certainly experience its advantages and instantly surpass our physical limitations.

Understanding how this energy is generated is not essential; what is crucial is that you can harness it and control this awesome energy.

You can become more familiar with this energy by using another example in this regard. You must have encountered situations in wrestling where you were behind in points, time was running out, you were exhausted, and you had abandoned your chance of winning. In this situation, something occurs unintentionally that causes you to immediately and unconsciously perform a technique that you would not have been able to implement under normal conditions, and as a result, you collect points, alter the situation in your favor, and ultimately triumph. This could be a strong voice from your coach, or it could be seeing or hearing a voice from another individual who has transformed your condition, or it could be a remembrance of your current problems. How was it possible that when you no longer had the energy to continue functioning, all the universe, the earth, and time conspired to ensure your success?

Absolutely, this is the same shock or, from a scientific standpoint, mental energy that has helped you and altered the condition. Your decision is influenced by the signals received from your environment via your five senses, which may have external and environmental, or internal foundations, including the employment of your memory and mental information repository.

What exactly is mental preparation?

Mental preparation refers to the process of strengthening and preparing the soul and mind to accomplish a specific objective. The success of an athlete is often attributed to their mental preparation, which is a multifaceted and expansive process. Without this type of preparation, athletes are unlikely to be successful. This preparation is essential for success, and athletes who are more motivated and mentally prepared will perform better in their competitions. In other words, mental preparation serves as an athlete's physical driving engine on the competition field. Wrestlers put in a lot of work and stress to reach the pinnacles of achievement, just like other athletes do throughout their athletic careers. However, these numerous and lengthy attempts and workouts are not feasible without a spirit and an objective, and the outcome is predictable from the beginning. The appropriate spirit and solid mental preparation are prerequisites for achievement and the complement to winning in competing fields. Fitness on the physical and mental levels is like two parallel lines moving together.

What is mental preparation, and how does it occur?

Your eagerness to complete a function and pursue a particular objective constitutes this mental preparation. Its emergence and formation are influenced by a component termed self-confidence. Many variables influence self-confidence, including family and its different dimensions. Community and its surroundings, genetics. In general, our self-confidence is directly impacted by any source of influence.

But our mental filters, which directly affect our emotions and shape our self-confidence, are the key actors in this aspect.

What is self-confidence?

Self-confidence, which is shaped by our mental filters, is a degree of self-belief.

Several factors are the sources of these mental filters, including family, society, economy, culture, politics, and even genetics. These factors have been discussed, and you now understand what mental filters are and how to deal with them

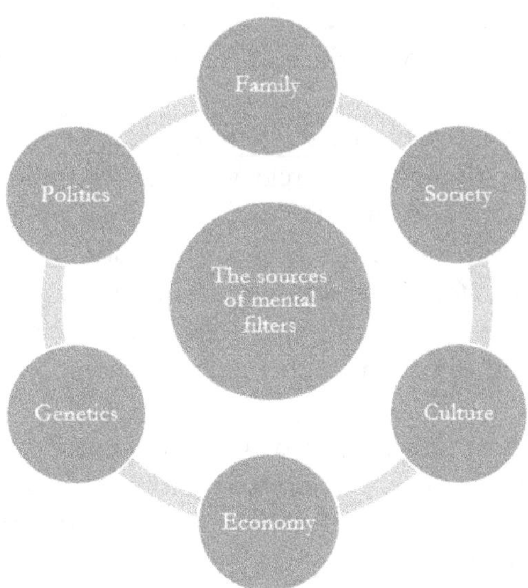

Family

The first institution where you grow up and develop is your family, and it has a very strong influence on your thoughts. The foundation of your personality and the core of your views are both developed there. This institution reflects your thinking style and seeing the universe, and it has an important role in the development of your self-confidence. Several family factors influence your level of self-confidence, including the family's economic level, political, cultural, and social ideas and tendencies, geographic location, parental education level, and even inheritance. Your self-confidence will be immediately impacted by these factors, which will also somewhat change your personality. These will demonstrate whether you have adequate confidence. Your family is where you initially develop your mental filters for all life aspects. It is of the utmost importance and vitality that your vision is either positive and full of self-confidence or negative and lacking in self-confidence. Athletes' and wrestlers' success or failure is heavily influenced by their families.

Society and community

You enter the community, which serves as the second base, and you begin to naturally absorb effects from this environment. It contributes to the development of your personality, as well as your self-belief and self-confidence, although not to the extent of your family. This environment sends you pulses and feedback, whether positive or negative, that can influence your behavior and mentality and impact your mood and thoughts. Suppose the mentality and thoughts of the community in which you live are positive. In this case, it is only natural that these views will have an impact on your condition and encourage you to adopt a positive outlook and alter your flawed mental filters. You will naturally remove erroneous mental filters in this condition. On the other hand, if the society in which you live is prejudiced and engaged in negative ideas, these thoughts will affect you and you will become like the society unless you possess a weapon known as mind control.

This can affect the athletes' morale and self-confidence, and it won't be ineffectual in helping them develop their personalities. Additionally, wrestlers and sportsmen live in this setting, interacting with it frequently on a regular basis and absorbing both positive and negative impacts from society. This prevailing worldview can be found in all aspects of society. As a result, an athlete must be able to handle and control this social phenomenon in order to reap its advantages while avoiding its drawbacks. In other terms, he ought to be able to exercise mental control and management on the ideas received from the surrounding community.

Example

If you are a wrestler living in a community where you are continuously bombarded with negative ideas and pulses, and these thoughts encircle you and cause you to lose confidence, you must concentrate on your thoughts and mindset. Additionally, you should manage these thoughts in accordance with your mental filters, adopt an optimistic outlook, and eliminate any negative thoughts. You should pay greater attention to your aim in this case and block out any unfavorable thoughts. These unfavorable ideas and pulses are always present, but you must adjust them according to your filters and direct them in a good orientation to achieve the ideal attitude and mental preparedness.

It should be recognized that doing so needs work and repetition and that training the mind takes time, just like training the body. One must exercise and constantly work to develop excellent mental fitness, just like one does physical fitness. As a result, one should first identify the flaws and afterward take corrective action.

Archive of memory and information

The impact of memory and information archives on wrestling technique and tactics:

As previously stated, our mind's memory and information archive are responsible for keeping and storing the information and data that have already been acquired by our minds. Thus, in wrestling and while discussing technique and tactics, our mental memory plays a crucial role. Since our minds work in accordance with the arguments provided and previous learning, they would not function otherwise. It makes previously learned data accessible when required. These previous and cumulative learnings and data can now be positive and beneficial or negative and erroneous. Memory's responsibility is to make earlier data accessible. Therefore, the knowledge and information we have given our thoughts can directly influence the technique and tactics. The significance of our mind's memory is decided by the given material. Have we supplied proper or erroneous information to our memory during the technique discussion? If we have provided our memory and mind accurate and valuable information, they will apply it when appropriate, and the outcome will be acceptable. However, if we have provided our memory with erroneous and incorrect data, the outcome is obvious.

It is crucial that we store accurate and logical knowledge in our memory while discussing techniques since this is where accurate and principled learning come into play and how to employ them is crucial. This is critical to our right and rational learning. We will surely be more successful if we learn the skills appropriately and with greater comprehension. In this situation, we will prevent the issue of going back and modifying the technique, which will also take time. As a result, it is preferable and more reasonable to acquire the techniques from the initial stage in a more fundamental and logical manner since we will unavoidably present anything we learn.

The discussion of tactics follows the same pattern, and we will offer the strategies we have already learnt, whether they are sound and appropriate or not. It is obvious that we will obtain empirical perceptions of techniques through time and adopt them, whether correct or incorrect. If it is correct, we will gain, but if it is incorrect, we will incur losses, and it may take us a long time to discover our mistakes and attempt to rectify them. This alteration and rectification can be achieved by experience or by obtaining the appropriate information and awareness, and our mind and memory will not function otherwise.

Learning and memorizing will develop after exercise, and it is important to recall anything accurate and reasonable.

Understanding something is the best method to learn and remember it. It is vital to study that subject from all perspectives, which can include learning approaches or tactics. It is undeniable that you can repair a problem over time by obtaining the essential experience and insight and by eliminating your mental locks; nevertheless, this method is expensive and time-consuming. Experience is a bad teacher, whereas knowledge and thinking are good teachers.

There are several approaches to achieving the ideal mind:

Using studying, good and strong coaching, expert consultants, and also changing the geographical environment to learn and experience, initiating to alter negative thoughts, rejecting negative mindsets, making negative thoughts positive, entering positive-thinking communities and getting motivation, cutting the connection to negative people, good and suitable mental imagery, watching motivational videos, practicing mind control, yoga, and meditation, etc., are effective in obtaining the awareness and correct information. There are countless practical and productive techniques to train and manage the mind.

Last line: Your thoughts are the foundation of everything you accomplish or achieve. The circle of knowledge and awareness in your mind shapes your performance. Hence, it is of the utmost importance that you enhance your knowledge and information in your field of exercise or attempt to gain experience and knowledge from them. The latter will be more challenging, and you will either have to pay the cost or spend a lot of time and energy to accomplish it. The decision is yours.

It should also be mentioned that your five senses are at the base of everything happening for you. These five senses receive the happenings in your environment and transmit them to your mind. According to your mental filters, your mind determines what to do and how to react to an incident. All of the information has been archived and kept in your mind. If you recall, it was explained at the beginning of this chapter that the mental structure is made up of memory and information archive, memory management, memory arrangement, and body management.

It is critical to understand how your body reacts and responds when you are wrestling. When you practice or adopt techniques or tactics, your mind classifies and organizes these techniques and tactics workouts in its archive and memory. When required, it eventually makes it accessible for you. For your mind to store these techniques and tactics in memory and make them accessible when needed, it is crucial that you practice all of the techniques and tactics, along with all of their details. If we wish to delve deeper, we must acknowledge that each cell in our body possesses the memory capacity known as cellular memory.

If you want to maintain strong morale and mental preparedness at all times, you must rectify your thinking and eliminate negative mental filters. Hence, developing awareness, receiving accurate and logical information, gaining experience, and exercising mental self-control and thought management are the only ways to get rid of harmful mental filters. This includes mental preparedness. Knowing the source and foundation of one's problems helps one deal with them better and more logically, avoid side paths more often, and find solutions to difficulties more quickly.

Everyone should have their unique version in terms of mental preparation and acquisition due to the breadth of human mental dimensions and the variances between human minds. It is impossible to employ the same approaches and techniques to boost morale and motivation for everyone all of the time. Since persons differ regarding information and awareness (mental filters), and because these differences are continually developing. Because people have varied mental dimensions and awareness and information, it is not acceptable to employ several options to inspire the athlete. So, rather than a prescription for the athlete and using techniques to elevate the spirit of the athlete and wrestler, it is desirable to rectify the athlete's thinking more fundamentally and weed it out. Alternatively, we should teach athletes to understand their minds and how to control and govern them so that they can manage their mental and emotional situations.

Psychological crises management

All athletes who have competed in championship competitions have undoubtedly encountered difficulties and crises during their athletic careers and are somewhat accustomed to them, whether before, during, or after the games. They are well aware that athletes occasionally experience crises and incidents that are unexpected and challenging to forecast before, during, or after the competition. However, it is unavoidable and does occur on occasion; therefore, it is vital to confront and accompany it. The emergence of these crises and typically unanticipated circumstances will also impose psychological burdens on our athletic lives, as well as on our psyche and mindset. It is unquestionable that these events will happen, and sometimes they will turn out well for us and sometimes they will work against us.

The key point is how to respond to the incidence and what happens when these crises arise, not whether these occurrences happen or not.

During the course of an athlete's championship sport, crises typically fall into three categories:

1. Pre-match crises, which are frequently predictable.
2. Unpredictability of crises during competitions.
3. Post-competition crises

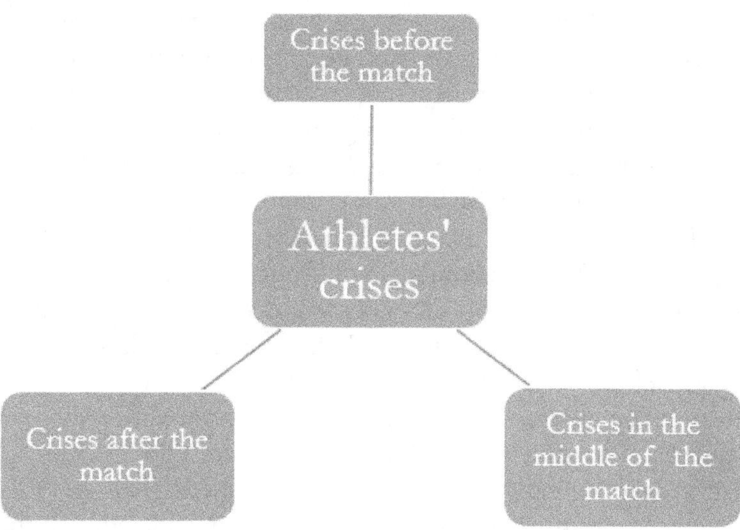

Each of these crises has the potential to directly impact our spirits and psyche as well as our athletic performance. As a result, it is critical to be informed of them so that when they arise, we can cope with them more rationally and prevent making wrong or irrational decisions.

As we are all aware, our physical health and performance are directly and closely related to our psyche and spirit. Both of these advance together and resemble parallel lines.

Thus, being in good mental and spiritual health can help us avoid the rough waters and storms of crises and guide us to the shore of serenity. If not dealt with and resolved, each of these crises will surely cause us to experience psychological and even physical difficulties that will hinder our ability to perform well in sports both during and after competitions.

1. Pre-competition crisis
Weight loss crisis, injury/sports injury crisis, inadequate sports facilities, and insufficient preparation time are all examples of this type of crisis.

Each of the factors mentioned above might have an impact on our mental and emotional conditions, diverting us from our purpose. Nearly all of us are also aware that these kinds of crises are foreseeable, allowing us to take a position on the situation and reach a thoughtful decision. This ensures that our spirit and mind are not adversely influenced by the competition.

2. Competition-related crises
These types of crises are usually unanticipated and unexpected, and they frequently arise during competitions. The mental and emotional states of the athlete during competition are most affected by this kind of crisis. Due to the elevated heart rate, low oxygen levels, and pressure on the body's muscles in this set of crises, mental decisions are more likely to be made incorrectly. If the athlete is unable to psychologically regulate and manage these crises and occurrences while competing, he will likely encounter major obstacles that will obviously be destructive to the athlete.

Crises during the competition
These encompass the crises of referee complaints, the crisis of injuries, the crisis of blackmailing spectators, the crisis of electrical stopwatch and camera malfunctions, and crisis of inconsistent tournament implementation. You may suffer psychological consequences if you experience any of these disruptions in the wrestling match. Occasionally these interruptions will be to your advantage, and sometimes they will be to your disadvantage. Ultimately, these unforeseeable incidents may occur throughout your competition and cannot be avoided. More essential, to pass these crises successfully, the athlete must be able to conduct mental control and management.

If we intend to proceed even further, we must admit that these disruptions in the wrestling process are sometimes purposeful and artificial. Taking a short break to achieve a certain objective and altering the wrestling circumstances is a form of tactic used to progress the individual's or coach's predetermined goals. For instance, purposefully pausing the wrestling to slow down the opponent's wrestling rhythm or simulating an injury for relaxation and physical recovery.

"Winning and defeat in confrontations begin in people's minds, whether they assume themselves triumphant or defeated."

The process of mental preparation development
1. Diagnosis: For any work, we must first obtain a correct diagnosis. We will surely run into issues and experience difficulties with our operation if, for any explanation, we are unable to correctly diagnose the problem. If we can't establish a correct diagnosis, we'll have a hard time assessing and displaying our work and practice. This translates to futile labor. Accordingly, in the psyche and spirit diagnosis, we must first establish and comprehend where the person's mentality is wrong and deficient, and subsequently, we may address other concerns. We can learn to some extent the psychological generalities of the athlete and identify the issues by examining the person's emotions and behaviors or by performing psychological evaluations and putting them together.

2. Analysis: After obtaining access to the athlete's moods and emotions, we must evaluate and determine the source of these benefits and drawbacks, as well as the main reason for these behaviors. We also need to understand how these circumstances impacted the athlete's performance. Does the person's family or the community in which he lives have a role in his mental health issues? All factors, including economy, culture, religion, community, friends, family, and so on, should be assessed to identify the above difficulties.

3. Solution: After we've identified the underlying cause of the person's lack of morale and mental preparedness and have controlled the person's mental state, we must supply a solution and develop a strategy. In addition, we must develop a solution to each of the potential concerns so that our efforts are not futile. We must provide solutions at the familial, social, and economic levels, depending on the type of problem.

4. Exercise: Now is the moment to address the problems, or if they demand mental and spiritual activity, consider workouts for them. That is because the athlete can discard the erroneous and negative mindset of his past and move forward with a fresh and correct mentality while still making advancement in his profession.

Chapter 4

Tactics and strategy

Introduction

Before talking about strategy and tactics, we need to be informed of their existence and significance in the competition so that we may make the best choices possible and stay on the right path.

Strategy and tactics are two crucial and vital components in achieving athletic objectives, which sportsmen must understand and prioritize to avoid becoming passive and weak along the complex journey to the championship.

What is the strategy?

In actuality, numerous interpretations and definitions of strategy have been proposed, all of which are broadly similar; however, there are different viewpoints in their details, making it impossible to establish a single description. We'll attempt to explain these concepts in this chapter.

In its broadest sense, strategy is determining the technique of achievement over a specific time period, or it is adopting broad decisions in order to attain long-term objectives. In order to reach the intended objectives in the field of the championship with work and effort, it is excellent and desirable for athletes and wrestlers to set a clear and distinct path for themselves at the commencement of their championship journey.

What is the tactic?

Tactics refer to various methods and tactics to obtain victory on the battleground against adversaries. In other terms, it can involve performing a succession of short-term acts in order to reach a specified goal while competing.

Two crucial and evident characteristics of tactics are typically present: a wide range of tactics, speed of changing tactics

There are numerous types and forms of tactics, and they are so versatile that they can be altered or abandoned rapidly. Tactics are successful as long as the conditions permit, and they should be replaced when they lose their effectiveness. Despite a definite and defined strategy, the conditions and scenario of the type of tactics used will often inform us when and where to switch tactics.

There is a strong correlation between a wrestler's IQ and his or her tactics, which originate directly from the athlete's mind and thinking. Wrestlers with the active minds are often tactical.

Tactics are classified into two categories in the field of wrestling and other individual fighting sports:
1. General tactics
2. Detailed tactics

General tactics

These are the tricks and tactics employed during a wrestling match to keep the existing condition or to shift the path of the battle. There are two types of tactics: defensive tactics and attacking tactics.

Defensive tactics

They are activities and behaviors undertaken by wrestlers in order to maintain the existing condition in wrestling. They are also known as controlling wrestling, and wrestlers employ them frequently to achieve the favored results.

Attacking tactics

They are a set of acts designed to interrupt competitors' concentration and tactics on the battlefield in order to achieve victory. Some of them encompass the tactic of repeatedly attacking in order to exhaust the opponent physically and emotionally, among others.

Detailed tactics

When fighting with opponents, detailed tactics refer to the employment of small tricks. In simpler words, they are the wrestling-specific details that most wrestlers are somewhat acquainted with. In general, they are the same agreements that we make when engaging in combat to win points or keep the outcome.

One of the most crucial-or, if it is not an exaggeration, one of the core components-of the five foundations of wrestling is tactic. Wrestling's most exciting aspect is its tactics, and the sport would be meaningless without them, according to the latest version of wrestling that has taken hold around the world. If the wrestlers are uninformed of this section, there will be no progress. Wrestlers in today's world wrestling system have advanced to a high level of competition and have a wealth of information and expertise concerning the sport. Wrestling, as in the past, is no longer centered on physical power and force, according to contemporary facilities, and participants have a greater understanding of the sport. The majority of athletes have studied and are familiar with the details of wrestling; thus, victory in this sport does not solely depend on having a strong technical field. They are in excellent physical condition when competing, and in wrestling, being in the excellent physical condition and having a good technical level are solely seen as required instruments. They should therefore be owned by every wrestler. In modern world-class wrestling, the advantage of these tactics is that they determine who wins most of the time, particularly in close fights where both combatants are of the same level and wrestling grade. It should be acknowledged that wrestling has changed significantly from the past, both in terms of its overall design and in terms of the achievement criteria and factors. It's not like before when wrestlers mostly used their physical prowess and skills to win competitions. Everything has altered, and wrestlers are no longer readily vanquished or tolerant of any technique. Presumably, to succeed, they will have to employ a variety of tactics.

As a result, this crucial and vital category should be approached differently, and new tactics and tactics should be learned and utilized to achieve success. Wrestlers will obtain outcomes in terms of fighting tactics after wrestling for a long period and participating in numerous tournaments. However, it can take years of empirical training before we become tactically skilled. We only become aware of these things after squandering a lot of time, at which point we also comprehend that it is too late and that our athletic careers or the time for working out and wrestling are finished. It is unusual to come across people who learn these skills during a youth period and benefit from them. We describe these concepts, and you should try to include them in your wrestling. In this situation, you can join the tactical wrestlers and cut the path to success short. In order to explain this matter more succinctly, we must state that in the contemporary world of professional wrestling, achievement and defeat are decided on more than one level by the fighting tactics. We expect that by now, you understand the significance of this issue and that wrestling is more than just using strong arms and good technique. Other factors contribute to its effectiveness. They can ensure your achievement in large fields.

There are numerous components to learning combat tactics in order to be regarded as a competent tactician wrestler, such as analysis, management, stylistics, design, and planning

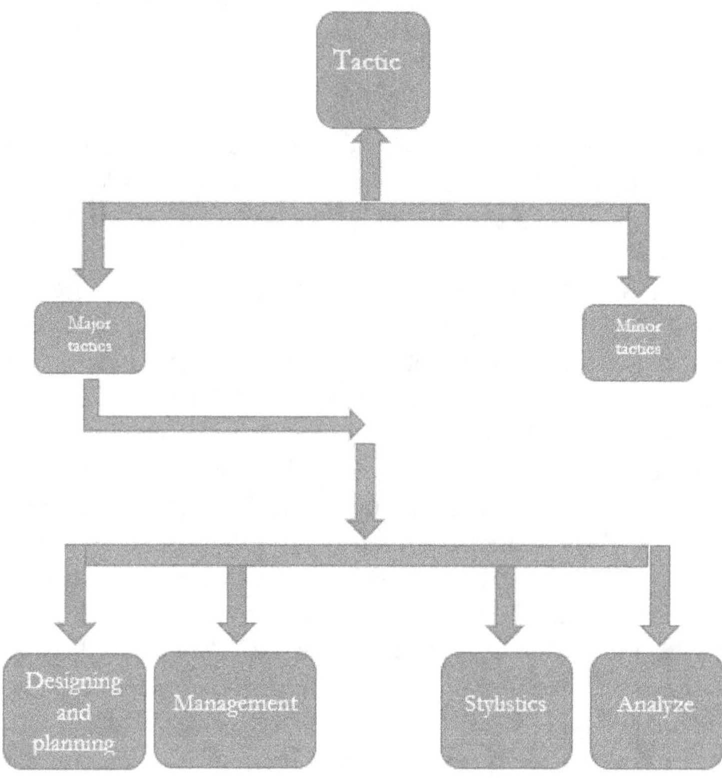

What exactly is analysis?

In order to execute a full and comprehensive analysis, numerous dimensions and perspectives must first be recognized and categorized. Wrestling has numerous components that must be evaluated, including technical, tactical, physical, and psychological, which will be discussed further below.

Analyzing entails evaluating, identifying, and categorizing the strengths and weaknesses from all angles and delivering an appropriate work solution

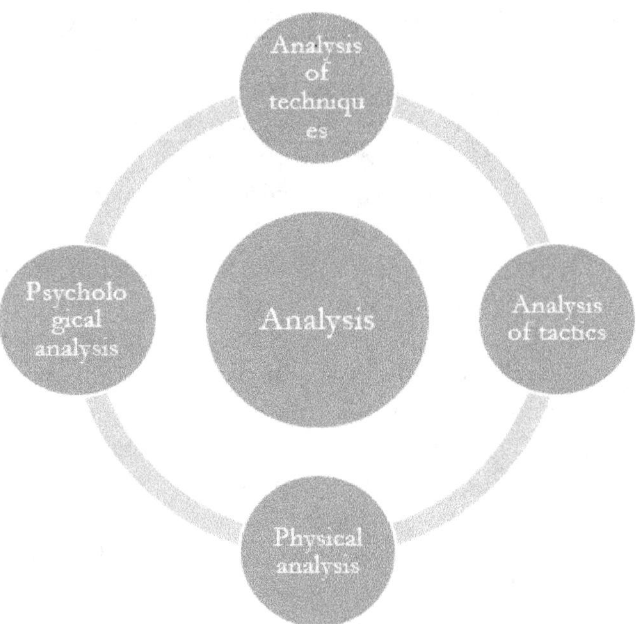

Analyzing is a modern and widespread practice in today's sports, and it is employed by all sports' technical personnel. They receive a wealth of knowledge from other opponents by acquiring such information, which can be helpful and beneficial in their achievement and triumph journey. As previously stated, to provide a correct analysis and comprehension of the current situation, it comprises numerous components of technical, tactical, physical, and even psychological analysis. The purpose of this analysis can be to identify the wrestler's talents and inadequacies. Depending on our wants and aspirations, it might also be an opponent analysis.

Technical analysis:

Technical analysis is the process of evaluating a competitor's technical position in terms of the sort of execution techniques employed by the opponent.

For instance, you would initially observe the techniques used by an opponent when attempting to assess his condition. In this situation, you attempt to comprehend the approaches your opponent uses to attack or, conversely, the strategies he employs to defend. This attention to your opponent's activities when implementing techniques is simply referred to as evaluating the opponent's technique in order to cope with your potential attack. This approach of analysis is more or less well-known to everyone. It only takes a close glance to observe the orientations of your opponent's wrestling and to be able to "read" the wrestling. Analyzing and observing properly has its own set of principles and regulations, and you must consider many things and plan accordingly, including the type of technique execution method, how to begin technique execution, time, and execution time, technique, physical factors of technique execution, and so on. After learning about these aspects and considerations, you should make a conclusion and offer a solution for each discovered factor.

Tactic analysis:

The tactic, as the name implies, comprises ways and methods of fighting, as well as the use of tactics and tricks when competing and wrestling to obtain points or maintain the outcome. Tactic analysis, to put it in much simpler terms, is the analysis of the tactics employed by opponents during combat. For instance, using tactical knowledge, you may comprehend the answers to the following questions: Where should you attack in wrestling? Where should defense work be carried out? Where should we rest during the wrestling? Where should the wrestling's rhythm be slowed down? Where should you accelerate? With which wrestler should you wrestle with strength?   as well as other instances

You must have several plans in place during the competition, from the beginning to the finale. As stated, the tactics can be altered rapidly, and you can employ them as long as the situation permits. Your current tactics won't work as the situation evolves; therefore, you'll need to use a new one to accomplish your objectives. You must have the appropriate instruments for this, including excellent physical fitness, good and advantageous technical abilities, and tactical variety so that you can consistently follow your plans and objectives because these plans can alter at any time. In some circumstances, if you are informed of good and appropriate tactics, you can even disguise your physical and technical limitations by employing them.

Wrestling tactics and scheduling are more essential and vital in today's world than other wrestling parts; if not hyperbole, other wrestling parts are essential subsets and instruments of this area. High physical fitness, a strong technical base, and high mental fitness cannot be the solution to your performance if you are unable to take full advantage of this issue. These tools might be effective in very simple wrestling, but you won't have much luck using them in difficult or equal wrestling or at high levels.

Example:

You surely remember the Mr. Parviz Hadi's wrestling competition against his Georgian opponent Petraishvili at the Hungarian World Championship in 2018. In that competition, Parviz hadi exhibited a high degree of preparation and a good spirit; however, he was vanquished because he could not resist the tactics and alertness of fatigued Petraishvili.

Wrestling time management, technique management, tactical management, mental and psychological management, energy and physical factors management are all aspects in which an intelligent and tactical wrestler should be able to manage himself.

The management of the listed factors, which can make the athlete a pioneer in this sector, is one of the aspects that cause achievement in the discussion of tactics. Possessing a variety of tactics and being tacticable by athletes are essentially what differentiate wrestlers apart from one another and determine their ranking and grade at high levels and world classes. Regrettably, in our nation, this topic is little mentioned, or there is insufficient awareness for coaches to handle it. Throughout the year, the activities are largely centered on repetitive wrestling workouts or entail physical preparation practices, and tacticalness workouts are not undertaken. As previously stated, they frequently strive for great physical fitness and technical proficiency, and they are ignorant of this critical and vital topic. Wrestlers devote the majority of their time to the mat and practicing physical activities, and they devote less time to training wrestling tactics. They generally understand and experience this difficulty to some level owing to the time passage and the expenditure of a great deal of energy.

Physical analysis or fitness

According to the visual recording and analysis displayed in the battles, physical analysis refers to learning about and understanding the opponent's physical state, including learning about the opponent's body composition and the degree of physical preparation. Another definition includes understanding the opponent's weaknesses and strengths, as well as analyzing the amount of physical preparation and its variables. We must examine and analyze our opponent's preparation visually because we do not have knowledge of the level of preparation. This gives us a partial understanding of our opponent's level of physical preparation. Although this cannot be correct or fundamental, it cannot be without elegance, and at the very least, it provides us with general knowledge concerning our opponent's physical state. We also learn about some aspects of our opponent's physical preparedness and can plan accordingly.

Energy management

Energy management in wrestling entails a wrestler being informed of his physical state and level of physical preparedness, as well as knowing in which physical preparation variables the wrestler has strengths and weaknesses. After learning about his physical condition and gathering information about it, he should organize and design his wrestling accordingly, not wasting energy in fruitless so that he does not become weak and fatigued during the battle. He should be aware of his tolerance level, and expend and manage his energy cautiously. This is due to the fact that the energy expended when fighting is restricted and cannot be easily restored and regenerated. It appears to take time for the body to recuperate depending on the type of energy and the intensity of our exercise. If you recall, energy generation devices were thoroughly detailed in the second chapter, which dealt with physical preparation. According to the type of our activity and the intensity of the time, each system producing energy in the body needs a certain amount of time to return to its natural state and recuperate.

So, the subject of time is essential here for two primary reasons: 1. the time allotted for a wrestling battle is restricted to six minutes, and 2. recovery time during the battle is minimal or non-existent. Since our body has a finite amount of energy and it takes time to regenerate, we cannot waste or use it inadvertently. This issue is directly related to our body's level of preparedness and informs us how much we are permitted to employ our physical preparedness factors to avoid fatigue.

It has been observed frequently that the wrestlers failed to regulate their energy during fight and competition, expended all of their energy, and became weak and exhausted; as a consequence, they lost wrestling.

Example: Take into account the wrestling fight between Mr. Hassan Yazdani and American Taylor. Yazdani started out well but quickly ran out of energy in the first half, unable to conserve it for the second half, and failed to control it, which led to his vanquishing against the American opponent.

Time Management

Time management entails the wrestler being aware of where he competes in terms of time, planning for it, and respecting his moments and time. For instance, he should be aware of how to use the wrestling's time to his advantage or in accordance with his strategies, including when to attack and when to relax or perform attacking options.

Time has an essential and critical role in a wrestler's achievement or failure, and its importance cannot be overstated. There are moments during the 6-minute competition when both athletes are battling and struggling for achievement that is referred to as active times. In the meantime, there are times throughout a battle that will be squandered, referred to as inactive times. They are regarded as a suitable opportunity for physical and mental recuperation for various reasons.

Technique management

An intelligent and skilled wrestler never uses all of his talents and strategies in a single match and constantly manages his numerous techniques. He uses skills and techniques depending on the type of requirements and circumstances in each fight, and he always has an alternative to use them when essential and mandatory. In other terms, he does not leave his fist open for his rivals, which prevents them from analyzing his performance strategies. Consider that by frequently employing one or more of your particular strategies, these performance techniques will become evident to everyone. Obviously, your rivals will examine your strategies and make it challenging for you.

Tactical management

Similar to technique management, tactic management requires that you occasionally refrain from using every tactic at your disposal. This is for the simple reason that your hand will be turned, and your work will become more challenging as a result of tactical analysis being performed on your state. A wise and tactical wrestler takes a variety of tactical plans and strategies and adapts his tactics, techniques, and tricks based on the situation so that he cannot be easily analyzed by his opponents. He has dominance and management over his executive tactics, and depending on the scenario, he immediately changes his tactics, despite the fact that evaluating tactics is a bit intricate and concealed, and it takes more time to examine them.

Psychological management

Mental management refers to a wrestler's capacity to control his feelings, psyche , and thoughts prior to, during, and after wrestling and competitions, such that emotions, stress, fears, and anxieties do not negatively impact the wrestler's performance. Because you are constantly confronted with positive and negative thoughts. If you recall, as extensively explained in this chapter's topic of mental preparation you receive pulses from your environment using your five senses, which can have an immediate impact on your mood and psychology. You must be able to predominate on these thoughts and environmental stimuli without allowing them to overwhelm your state. These thoughts or environmental currents should always be under your management, and you should manage them such that they have no impact on your performance or reduce them. Because of the fluidity of both positive and negative thoughts, which can penetrate through the environment to your mind or emerge through speech, you must manage them and, if you are unable to do so, engage in mental management. You will definitely lose concentration on the primary problem, which is the competition and wrestling, as a result of your poor mental management, and finally, you will defeat. Nowadays, there are numerous methods for controlling your thoughts and mind that you might employ to achieve this objective

Stylistics

Stylistics refers to the ability to categorize in terms of the opponent's fighting type. Another description of

stylistics includes understanding the type and style of opponents' fighting during wrestling. To comprehend the various sorts of wrestling styles, you must first understand them, then classify and explain them in order to recognize how to deal with them

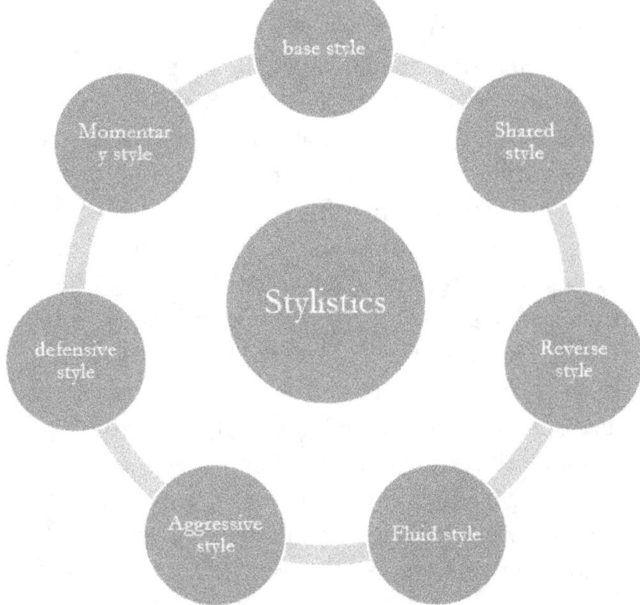

1. Common style
2. Reverse style
3. Attacking style
4. Defensive style
5. Floating style
6. Basic style

General stylistics

A skilled and competent wrestler must be knowledgeable about the fighting and wrestling styles of his or her opponents. He should not enter the mat without a plan and a strategy for dealing with the fighting style and type of his opponents. It may be conceivable to enter the mat without a strategy in light and easy wrestling and succeed, but this deficiency will be sensed in important and vital wrestling. As a result, learning all of the styles and incorporating them into the workouts is required in order to employ them when applicable.

Basic style

In a simple way, it can be said that the basic style includes the desired style and model that you choose for wrestling, and you can show your capabilities more conveniently. It can encompass all of the wrestling's styles. Style selection is determined by your physics type, level of physical preparedness, and mental and emotional conditions.

Reverse style

In general, wrestling against the desires or the basic style of the opponents is called the reverse style .In this way of fighting, one should not fight according to the opponents' desire. Implementing a reverse style can be one of the successful styles for dealing with opponents because it can be highly beneficial and fill in the gaps. This strategy requires you to select a wrestling style against your opponent after learning the type and style of their fight. It implies that when your opponent wrestles using any style, you should attempt to wrestle against that style and challenge your opponent so that he cannot simply accomplish his strategies. This necessitates the ability to wrestle using styles other than your basic and referencing styles. In other terms, do not dance to your rival's music, and do not fight according to his preferences. Since this form of battle challenges your opponent to reach his aims, leads him to become confused in his strategies, and causes him to lose concentration to some level, indicating a step forward for you.

It should be emphasized that in order to win a fight, you may require to demonstrate many styles of wrestling. Since it is impossible to be victorious solely by knowing the opponent's fighting style and employing a distinct fighting style from the opponent. Owing to the numerous ups and downs and abrupt changes in your opponent's wrestling technique, it is impossible to think about one type of combat and continue it ahead in wrestling. Therefore, to win the battle, your strategies must be constantly modified in response to the opponent's struggle and its present circumstances. To achieve your objectives, you must use a reverse wrestling style, but it doesn't imply your work is finished. This will simply complicate your opponent's strategies and serve as a challenge to your opponent. It's feasible that your opponent will have complete control over the match at any point. Your opponent must expend more energy and time in the reverse style to alter the situation to his advantage. In addition, he must expend greater time and effort in order to utilize his talents and techniques.

Common style

A common style is one in which both wrestlers have a lot of technical and tactical talents and battle in practically a similar manner.

It may appear simpler in wrestling when both opponents wrestle practically in a similar manner and have a common favored style. However, those who possess the wrestling details, high vigilance, high opportunism, and ability to combine speed with movement, as well as those who gain from high physical preparedness components, can triumph in this type of combat. There is also a chance that the match may be deadlocked, and you will need to use different aspects of wrestling to prevail.

Defensive style

This wrestling style is associated with defensive wrestlers who are less likely to engage in the attacking phase and exhibit less risk-taking ability. These people are so-called cautious and conservative, but they continue to attack compulsively. In this wrestling style and model, the wrestler concentrates mainly on the opponent's faults and always seeks to profit from the opponent's mistakes and gain points. Most of these wrestlers are skilled at managing their energy level and tactics, and they wrestle slowly. They primarily wait for their competitors' actions to respond and, in a sense, build a trap for their opponents to collect points. The majority of these wrestlers do not readily lose points, but they also do not quickly get points, and their wrestling generally has low fluctuation , and few points are exchanged. Their mental filters are at the heart of this concept and their wrestling style.

Attacking style

As the name implies, this wrestling style is exclusive to those athletes who actively seek to attack their opponents. To win, they don't wait for the occasion to display their reaction. They create opportunities and space to succeed, and they are not scared to attack and assault the opponent. They are also very capable of taking risks. This kind of wrestler typically scores a lot of points by numerous continuous attacks, as opposed to defensive wrestlers, who are frequently cautious and conservative and constantly wait for a mistake by their opponents to react and score. Regrettably, they frequently do not gain much from energy and tactical management, and they also lose a lot of points.

Floating style

This wrestling model and style is a blend of all the wrestling models and styles, such as the common style, reverse style, defensive style, and attacking style. This group of wrestlers is distinguished by their ability to perform well on both the defensive and attacking aspects. They may also change methods immediately in the face of competitors with a common style and can implement a reverse style effectively. In addition, rather than acting in a reverse manner, they adapt to and modify the circumstances, and they usually have strong knowledge and bravery. This class of wrestlers, similar to defensive wrestlers, does not lose points conveniently, and they can breach any competitor's barrier and get points. They can wrestle in all styles and have the traits of outstanding and world-class wrestlers based on the situation.

Weight classes

Decuple weights are separated into three categories in wrestling, including lightweight, middle weight, and heavy weight. Because of the different types of athletes' physiques, each of these groups has its own set of distinctions and traits.

Light weight category characteristics

Weight classes 57, 61, 65, and 70 are included in this category. This group's distinguishing qualities include their remarkable speed and agility, as well as their acceptable methods. Wrestling in this class has numerous ups and downs, and frequent points are exchanged within this group.

Middle weight category characteristics

Weight classes 86, 79, and 74 are included in this category. This category is a combination of two weight categories: light and heavy. To be successful in this category, a player must have both the characteristics and criteria of the lightweight and heavyweight categories. That implies, in this category, he must have velocity, agility, and excellent technique, as well as strong physical strength and tactical ability similar to like heavyweights. This division of wrestling is a little more challenging than the previous two types.

Heavy weight category characteristics

Weights 92, 97, and 125 are included in this category. High physical strength and employing good and acceptable strategies are two key qualities of this category. This category has less movement than other categories of wrestlers owing to their comparatively high weight, mobility, and lower speed, and the vast majority of the wrestling is dependent on physical strength and tactics.

Notes for introducing yourself to a range of styles

If you consider the wrestlers who fight aside from their opponents and participate in less combat with them, if you attempt to wrestle against them and go near them in this scenario, you will observe that your opponent will constantly attempt to separate himself and avoid engaging in combat. This is a reverse wrestling style, indicating a challenge for your opponent and a step ahead for you. This entails generating a unique chance if you are acquainted with different wrestling techniques, have experience with them, are skilled enough to compete in them, and can wrestle in a variety of styles. This opportunity and experience will come from wrestling and practicing a lot against many opponents, which will allow you to wrestle in a variety of styles rather than just one. It is abundantly evident that each wrestler has a reference style and that wrestler works with the style that he prefers the most and with which he feels convenience. A seasoned and conscious wrestler, on the other hand, does not disregard different forms of wrestling and understands and implements them when needed.   Since wrestling does not always proceed in your favor unless you are one of those wrestlers with a good capability compared to their opponent and can implement your style on them. In this situation, your opponents will constantly have to surrender to your floating wrestling style. You must have several characteristics for this sort of wrestling, and you don't be concern about how your opponent wrestles. This implies you must understand the four wrestling concepts of technique, tactics, physical preparedness, and mental preparation.

Exercising with various opponents and obtaining essential experience can teach you how to compete using different styles and make you more experienced. A crucial aspect, though, is that time and energy are wasted for nothing. Therefore, paying attention to these points and putting them into practice throughout training might make learning these abilities easier for you and save your time and energy.

Momentary stylistics

Momentary stylistics refers to the capacity to categorize and comprehend your opponent's battle and wrestling style in a brief period of time, usually in the initial seconds of wrestling competition with your opponent. It may have happened that you competed with unknown opponents. In this circumstance, you obviously did not have a strategy for dealing with them, and you sought to develop your wrestling and regular strategies, except your opponents are one of those wrestlers that you have fought with their style before, and you understand how to combat them mentally and empirically to some level. This is made possible by your extensive expertise and numerous matches with wrestlers of all styles. It may take several years to have sufficient experience to complete this assignment. This necessitates the expenditure of both energy and time. The character and style of your opponent's wrestling can be understood in the fight's initial moments and can help you avoid this challenge, which is a new strategy to help you achieve your goals.

In the initial moments of your match with your opponents, it is better to pay attention to their wrestling style. As a result, you will be able to classify their style, determine the type of wrestlers, and understand the factors behind their fighting style. This ought to be discussed and pointed out frequently by coaches so that you are aware of your opponent's general style and technique.

Another point for recognizing and distinguishing many different styles as much as possible:

Remember that, in general, wrestlers whose working process is advanced during the match and who exert more attempts can be classified as having an attacking style. A defensive style can be used to describe wrestlers who always want to engage in head-to-head combat, adhere to and hold their opponents, and slow down the pace of the match. Their diagnosis method is straightforward and comfortable.

Keep in mind that wrestlers exerting more effort and using more maneuvers in any region necessarily possess more skills and competence in that region.

Tactical growth process

1. Diagnosis: The best and most certain approach to improve and expand in any subject is to notice and acknowledge the issue from all angles that contribute to advancement.

We must first accurately diagnose our tactical strengths and shortcomings to have a clear road forward and be able to call ourselves tacticians and tactician wrestlers, as well as be successful in the field of tactics.

2. Analysis: After providing a correct diagnostic and recognizing the set of tactical components, we must now examine and investigate our tactics to clarify all of the positive and negative parts of our tactics. It should be established which tactical areas we are weak in and which tactical areas we have adequate tactics, both in terms of style and tactical management.

3. Solution: In the third stage, we should move on to the introduction of the solution and establish what should be conducted to make progress, as well as what approaches and methods should be employed to get rid of any inadequacies.

4. Practice: We will discuss training after accurately diagnosing our tactical issue, recognizing our tactical limitations and strengths, and proposing a precise and correct solution. At this moment, we practice the concepts learned in order to achieve success and advancement.

Chapter 5

Sports life management

Introduction

One of the five concepts and basis in today's wrestling that athletes and wrestlers should consider is sports life management. They should endeavor to follow it throughout their sporting careers so that they can navigate the challenges and difficulties of becoming a champion. They should be as meticulous with their athletic life as they are with their wrestling and other activities, and they should be able to handle and manage it. Since if you are unable to handle and manage this issue throughout the period when you are participating in championship competitions, your performance in championship sports will be tainted and will be more dependent on chance and fortune. Your life will surely require planning, just as it does in the world of sports and wrestling, so you should exercise caution in this regard. If you are unable to manage and govern your life in any manner while competing in championship sports, you will undoubtedly suffer a downturn in your sports and wrestling. Both have a direct relationship; therefore, if either of them has flaws or deficiencies, it will surely have an impact on your workout.

Since controlling an athlete's sporting life plays a significant and important role in the achievement or failure of that athlete's endeavors, this aspect should be carefully considered and followed so that the athlete can make the difficult road to the championship more convenient.

It has been demonstrated several times that there were numerous athletes and wrestlers who possessed the characteristics of an elite wrestler and everyone predicted a promising future for them, but the athlete confronted many obstacles since the wrestlers themselves or their families were unable to manage their athletic life. This will continue until life's concerns and obstacles involve the wrestler, and wrestling, and sports are relegated to the sidelines. In this situation, the athlete's light of hope will eventually fade until it turns off, and he will withdraw from the primary path to becoming a champion. Finally, he does not have much achievement in wrestling and so defeats. In order to make our path to achievement and a championship easier, we need to understand the significance of athletic life and how it should be managed. But what are the variables that might be important in this situation and directly affect an athlete's everyday life and performance outside of the wrestling match?

There are numerous aspects in the realm of sports life that contribute to or hinder success in professional sports. To help you understand their significance, we'll mention a few of them.

Understanding sociology, which is directly related to athletic life management, is necessary before we can proceed with the discussion of sports life management. This aids in understanding the meaning and concept of management in sports and in conducting an accurate analysis of the issue. Accordingly, by making proper and reasonable judgments in the future, we may make our journey to championship and professional sports life easier.

What exactly is sociology?

A science that explores and analyzes human life, as well as the activities and outcomes that take place in their social life, is called sociology. In other terms, it studies the overall qualities of society and the manner of social growth and development, as well as the social, political, economic, cultural, educational, and sporting relationships between humans.

The athlete can gain precise and comprehensive knowledge of the society in which he lives thanks to this analysis and study of that society. On the other hand, he can safeguard himself from the inconsistencies and erroneous decisions that occur in the course of his athletic life. In order to attain true achievement, an excellent and professional athlete must concentrate not only on his championship sport but also on his sports life and professional life.

In actuality, these peripheral aspects of our lives are examined and explored by the study of sociology. The frameworks and outcomes of our society are described for us by this science. Studying them allows us to draw conclusions about them and to understand their effects and consequences. Accordingly, we can safeguard ourselves against societal hazards, harms, and abnormalities while also leading a professional sports life. Numerous societal factors affect everyone's quality of life, wherever they may be in the world. A person's personality and, to some extent, their fate are determined by a combination of these factors. They are family, society, economy, culture, sports, politics, etc.

These aforementioned factors may have a direct impact on our athletic performance and pose a challenge to our exercise progress, or lack thereof.

Since an athlete is also a member of this big society on this planet. The performance of the sportsman might be significantly impacted by the aforementioned factors. As a result, we should be aware of these factors and incorporate them into our sporting lives, as well as regard them as a guiding concept in our exercise process rather than dismissing them.

One of these topics that have taken hold and developed quickly in the modern world is sports as a social phenomenon. Its pinnacle and most visible manifestation are the Olympic Games, which are athletic, social, cultural, political, and economic events. A nation's advancement and excellence in terms of politics, culture, society, and economy can be determined by its rank in the Olympic competitions. All countries are attempting to achieve success in this big sports area in order to showcase their country's growth and advancement to other countries. In fact, the Olympic arena resembles an economic, political, social, cultural, and sporting battleground. All countries are attempting to win this fight and demonstrate their country's advancement and development in all fields to other countries but in the guise of a beautiful, appealing, and attractive battle.

Now we return to the topic at hand, which is why we need management and control over the aforementioned factors in order to be successful. Underestimating and disregarding these issues what implications might have on our workout? You will learn more about this topic and how these aspects will play an outstanding role in our workout in the next sections. Geographic setting, family, society, economy, culture, and politics are some factors in a wrestler's sporting life.

These listed factors can have a significant impact on the development of an aptitude and be called a wrestler's achievement factor. Perhaps few people are aware of this issue, and they are often preoccupied with wrestling and its issues rather than the margins and other aspects of wrestling. However, it should be noted that controlling an athlete's sports life is unavoidable, and extra attention should be devoted for an aptitude to blossom and bears fruit. In many situations, this lack of attention to an athlete's life has forced the athlete to deviate from the primary road of his championship and has caused the player to encounter numerous difficulties. These circumstances have taught the athlete to overcome the issues and difficulties of his life, as well as his sports and wrestling.

It may be difficult for you to realize that environmental problems in wrestling have a substantial impact on an athlete's achievement and play a crucial role. But it must be acknowledged that managing and directing the athlete's sporting life is an equally important aspect of the work required to become a champion in wrestling and other sports. Both factors operate in tandem, and failure to pay attention to either will halt the athlete's progression.

This topic can be presented using an example to demonstrate the relevance of management in sports. This is a very important topic that deserves to be taken into account. If in your viewpoint, a wrestler possesses all the qualities of an elite wrestler but cannot govern and manage his social interactions, such as selecting friends and acquaintances and being associated with individuals who defy norms, he will surely suffer harm and be damaged.   In the future, he will likely be drawn to them. As a result, he will likely become one of the norm-breakers, deviate from his basic trajectory, which is playing sports and becoming a champion, and forget his direction.

Each of the factors mentioned above can impact your wrestling and your ability to become a champion. However, it is unavoidable that a person possesses all these factors according to the situations and factors mentioned. Perhaps it is uncommon to find someone with these positions. What then should be done? The fundamental issue here is that we all know that combining these factors is impossible and more akin to fantasy than actuality. We cannot possess all of these advantages, like a geographical location to reside in, a good family, good friends, or a stable economic status. However, we can fill and rectify these gaps to some level by attempting to manage and control these issues. We can properly handle our flaw so that it does not adversely damage our wrestling and sports.

All of us humans face problems and constraints. It is critical to understand how to cope with them, as well as how to control and manage them. Achievement and championship are not by chance but rather the result of a combination of external and internal factors. This also necessitates consciousness and insight, and fundamentally, every human being's misfortune and failure is founded on his lack of knowledge, which results in failure. Therefore, for success and advancement, we must expand our awareness and knowledge to fail less frequently or we need to have enough experience to realize that finding a solution to this problem will be time-consuming and expensive.

"Knowledge and being well-informed are excellent teachers, whereas experience is a bad teacher."

I wrote a hundred letters and demonstrated a hundred methods; either you don't read letters or you don't realize the way

However, how might the aforementioned factors affect whether we succeed or fail?

1. Geographical environment

Depending on where we live on the planet, we all experience distinct weather conditions, and this geographical environment can have diverse effects on us. For instance, the geographical location of our life can affect the way of our life, mood, and habits, as well as the type of race, genetics, culture, language, and many other factors.

The place and territory where we reside and grow up are reffered to our geographical environment. Undoubtedly, our mood, manner of thinking, and type of vision will be influenced by this territory's culture, climate, and economy. This is where our personalities will be formed in some way, and this is where the location's culture will overwhelm your thinking approach. Your genetic and body composition might be impacted by its climate. The region's economic status can have a significant impact on your routine life, and all of the factors mentioned above have an immediate impact on your condition.

For instance, migration may be an option to change the geographic setting in our favor and get rid of some of these factors. But the essential idea is that to gain positive feedback from these internal and external factors, one should endeavor to manage and control them. Presently, in your viewpoint, will an athlete be more successful if he is in an environment with these listed factors or in an environment that advantages less from these factors?

Do you believe an athlete who resides in a sports city is more successful than one who lives in a city where people struggle with addictions and other anomalies? The answer is unequivocal: we are affected by our surroundings. This is an instance of the influence of an athlete's geographical location on his or her athletic performance.

The athlete will definitely be more prosperous in an environment that is excellent and advantageous in all aspects. However, we all recognize that bringing all of these factors together is impossible, and it almost seems like a fantasy. Therefore, what should we do? Of course, we should take charge of the situation, keep it under control, and change it to our advantage.

2. Family

The family is the first center and community in which every human being is present, and it is from there that the initial environmental effects are received. The family is the source of the majority of effects that a person receives from various settings. Every human being's character and destiny, as well as his/her life and future strategy, might be built on the foundation of the family. In general, every human being's morality and individual values begin here.

The personality of the parents, their mental and emotional moods, the method of training children, economic and living situations, social communications, family culture, and other factors all play a role in the development of personality in the family.

These factors can encompass a person's work, sports, education, economic and social future, and to some extent, define a person's lifestyle and future. As the first community that can significantly impact us, the family is so crucial and extremely important. On the other side, family health may aid in any situation. In our conversation on wrestling sports and championships, we've established that family is the primary and most significant priority.

Factors stated in the family, including parents' personalities, financial status, and family culture, can significantly impact an athlete's performance and overwhelm an athlete's sporting life. Hence, it can be stated that the achievement of an athlete is dependent on the family , and one should be aware of this society. However, the athlete is unable to change his family or select an alternative. This problem is unavoidable and seems to depend more on your chance, your family, and where and when you were born. What should be done now? It is correct that you can't select your original family to be successful, and in reality, you don't have any alternative; nevertheless, if you raise your level of awareness and intellectual acumen, you can surmount this limitation to some degree. Seeking competent and compassionate advisors, as well as learning and boosting one's intellectual level, can all help in this field. It is possible to change the circumstance and create good and positive impacts on the family by managing and controlling the issue. You can also manage and change the situations to some extent after you attain intellectual maturity, and you can improve your conditions to the best possible level by adopting acceptable solutions.

3. Social relationships

Social relationships are developed as a result of how you communicate with the individuals in society and around you. Your regular interactions with others in society or the environment in which you reside will have an impact on you, as well as your thoughts and intellectual acumen. Positive or negative policies are received by your surroundings. These impacts can occur in a larger area, like your city, or in a smaller domain, like your group of friends and acquaintances.

However, our conversation focuses on how society affects athletes who aim to win championships, not how society affects an individual. Athletes' relationships with their friends and acquaintances greatly impact their achievement. As a result, good friends help the athlete attain his goal faster and avoid social anomalies. As a result, maintaining connections with friends is important in developing an athlete's personality and can be a strategy for himself. Therefore, it is crucial that we contact and communicate with friends and acquaintances with a high level of social health, as doing so can have favorable impacts on us.

4. Economy

Similar to the other three options, the economy can have a significant and fundamental impact on an athlete's performance. An athlete must be able to transcend his material constraints to succeed and achieve his objectives. As a result, it's crucial to be in a position of financial stability to cover sports-related requirements. In today's sports, the economy has a crucial and vital role for an athlete and overwhelms a wrestler's workout. In practice, it is impossible to exercise and attain objectives without these financial minimums. Athletes' mental and psychological performance can be improved to some amount, and they can also have some degree of mental tranquility, depending on their financial status. In this circumstance, the athlete cannot focus on his objective due to confusion, deficiency, and even lack of motivation caused by a lack of financial resources. One of the most important common dimensions humans are involved with is money and economic conditions. It is also a form of the necessity of contemporary existence; without it, people would be unable to meet their basic material necessities. As a result, having money and favorable economic circumstances can directly impact our quality of life and athletic performance. It is crucial to have a strong economy since it can impact our circumstances, as well as our mental and emotional states. This issue is increasing our reliance on this commodity on a daily basis, and all of our equations and interactions center around it. It is implicated in many of our relationships and even exercises.

To some extent, we are all informed of the significance of the economy, we have comprehended its important function, and we are aware that money and material items alleviate many of our difficulties. An athlete will immediately require this commodity to be a champion in his sporting life; without it, an athlete's sporting life will be challenged, and participating in sports will diminish it. These problems are likely to prohibit the athlete from participating in sports and becoming a champion. As a result, possessing a satisfactory economy and financial conditions is critical for an athlete. However, it should be noted that not everyone has access to enough financial and economic resources. This scenario is tied to various factors, including the fact that wrestlers often belong to lower social levels, and wrestling, in general, is more common in lower social classes. But how should athletes cope with and address this issue?

Again, the role of management emerges and demonstrates its relevance in sports life as well as its consequences on our exercise procedure.

It's possible that we are economically underprivileged, and having a strong economy and quality resources can help our sports in certain ways, but it's more crucial to handle and conquer this handicap so that it has less impact on wrestling and sports.

5. Culture

Another aspect that might be more effective on our personal or athletic performance is culture, which stems directly from our family, environment, and society. A society's general beliefs and behaviors are referred to as its culture. This society can be small, such as a family, or vast, like a city or even a whole country. The dominant culture of a region refers to a society's general habits and behaviors. This culture might now be positive and respectable, or it can be straggling and weak.

This prevailing culture of a place can significantly affect an athlete's sports performance and be inspirational. As a result, this issue should not be overlooked or dismissed.

Due to the fact that the collection of behaviors and mindsets of the society in which you reside will directly impact your performance and exercise, you must acquire cultural management skills.

Obviously, we cannot alone alter a society's culture. Generally, we are influenced by the culture around us. However, by increasing our consciousness and insight, we can alleviate some of the challenges and practice individual culture management, including studying, communicating with educated people, or selecting an excellent advisor.

6. Policy

Like the other factors listed, politics will have a significant impact on our workout. Politics, in general, refers to the process through which individuals develop legislation for their society. These established rules now have two possible outcomes: they can be beneficial and encourage social advancement and excellence, or they can be detrimental and cause society to suffer from flaws and shortcomings.

Similar to politics, these established regulations can have an effect on every member of society, including athletes who are members of the community.

7. Time

Yes, as previously stated, you need to plan for the issue of time and its management in addition to handling the previously discussed factors.

In essence, time management is split into two categories:

1. Time management on a daily and routine basis; 2. Long-term time management

Devoting the time to accomplish your heart's desire, like scheduling for the achievement established for yourself, frequently incorporates into three-time categories: short-term, medium-term, and long-term scheduling and goal setting.

Time management is the ability to be sensitive to the time allotted.

We are all aware that championship sports have a specific time frame that occurs only once in our life span and cannot be repeated. Because of our age situations, as we get older, we will no longer be eligible to have the same conditions as before in terms of our physical state. Time management is thus critical since it is irreversible, no one can experience it again, and it can only be slightly postponed.

1. Daily time management

Daily time management refers to the process of setting objectives and determining specific times for our circadian sports and non-sports activities. For instance, it could be mentioned while participating in sports, relaxing, pursuing education, a profession, or entertainment.

2. Long-term time management

Long-term time management refers to the amount of time an athlete regularly plans and devotes several years to achieve the top of the championship.

You cannot always take advantage of the championship period, as it is a brief and unpredictable time frame. The impacts of increasing years will become apparent, and the athlete's physical and mental health will determine how long the championship period will last. The length of this period is determined by a number of factors. As a result, time is critical. We all have a finite, almost specific amount of time to fulfill our wishes and achieve our objectives, and in order to do so, we must plan in accordance with that limited period of time.

According to scientists and experts, to achieve the level of a world-class professional athlete, 10,000 hours of training time are required. This entails approximately 20 hours of training per week and approximately eight years of effective and correct training with a schedule in order to reach the level of professional athletes. This requires devoting time. Why should we manage our time according to these numbers?

8. Sports injuries management

You are well aware that there is a risk of injury to one's body when engaging in any physical activity, including exercising. This is unavoidable, and for anyone who has exercised, this has occurred numerous times. The majority of the athletes are acquainted with this condition and have experienced it numerous times, enduring minor and major damages. However, more professional athletes are aware of and have experienced this problem more frequently.

Sports damages and injuries suffered by athletes while training or competing have two components: physical damage and emotional and psychological damage. These injuries, depending on their severity and extent, can have large and minor effects on the athlete, making the person's professional activity difficult and insufficient.

However, the occurrence or non-occurrence of damages and injuries is not the topic of our discussion. Since this is unavoidable and can occur at any time, putting an individual in jeopardy. Although they can be reduced with appropriate and basic scheduling and exercises, they are usually inevitable.

The objective of this section, however, is to identify, manage, and conquer physical and psychological injuries. It is essential to traverse this transition period in such a manner that the athlete's sports and professional exercises are not interrupted for too long.

Athletes who sustain sports injuries must also deal with mental and psychological harm in addition to their physical harm, depending on the type and extent of the injury. Sometimes an athlete suffers more severe mental and emotional damage than actual physical damage. These conditions lengthen the individual's recovery and reversibility process, both physically and psychologically, and may even be irrevocable. Here, the importance of management and control in preventing sports-related injuries is evident.

Two important and crucial points must be observed in some serious and important injuries, which are frequently deep incidents, and their treatment process is time-consuming: 1. When an injury occurs, proper and timely first aid should be provided; 2. Mental health and psychological care should be provided throughout the treatment period until thorough recovery.

It implies that, first and foremost, when an injury occurs, we can take advantage of the golden time and take the first stages to preclude additional damage to the damaged site. Among these measures are the application of ice compresses, the fixation of the damaged limb, bandaging, and so on. In the second stage, during treatment, we can perform routine workouts to keep our bodies in some degree of maintenance and keep them from collapsing, allowing us to return to the fields and recover without losing any time.

We can keep our spirits and motivation up during the recovery and treatment period. As a result of the fact that, when a person sustains a physical injury, he or she suffers a mental injury, is initially shocked, and thereafter tolerates the injury. In the third stage, he considers treatment after accepting the problem and damage, and this stage of acceptance and treatment is critical. During this time, a person usually experiences mental weakness and failure, as well as a loss of motivation or feelings of frustration. He is concerned that he will be neglected, that no one will accept him, and that interactions with him will become burdensome. The individual who was an enthusiastic and optimistic athlete before the injury becomes a disappointed and depressed person as a result of the above-mentioned behaviors, which have a negative impact on his morale. Hence, it's crucial to manage and take care of himself during the injury's transition period, both mentally and physically.

Undoubtedly, you also recall the athletes who, upon returning to competition after a lengthy injury, suffered a significant drop and were unable to demonstrate their former performance. Ensure that the athlete cannot successfully complete the treatment and recovery period. Since he is experiencing physical and mental vulnerability during his recovery period, this is due to avoiding physical exercises, discontinuing exercises abruptly, or losing his morale during treatment. Due to a lack of management and control over sports injuries, athletes have performed poorly and inappropriately upon their return to competition.

It has frequently been observed that athletes who suffer severe injuries and miss competitions are never able to recreate their prior performance and skills when they return to the fields. In fact, these individuals were unable to manage and control the duration of their injury, and when they returned, they encountered weakness and a lack of achievement as well as confusion. The failure to manage during the recovery period led to this lack of achievement. That is, they have failed to conduct physical activities or have abandoned entirely from the period of injury until the recovery. Maybe the nervous pressures induced by the damage overcame the athlete and conquered his morale, and the individual encountered a big shock when he returned.

Again, we are confronted with the management issue; specifically, what is management, and how should it be realized? Exercise is a part of management, the process used to address the issues and challenges faced in life. It is important to understand that no person is complete and that everyone has flaws in their lives. It is critical to recognize, manage, and pursue reconstructing these challenges. There are numerous means by which we can overcome economic, family, or social issues, etc. It is crucial to identify them in a short time and make an effort to control them rationally so that they do not significantly affect our athletic performance. Since our incapability to manage our sports lives will prevent us from fully expressing our strengths. Perhaps the absence of management in our sporting lives causes us to discontinue exercising.

A specific goal that provides someone with the motivation needed to surmount these issues and succeed is one of its solutions or the most crucial management technique. We've always attempted to explain these issues in depth rather than continuously command and forbid, point out the dos and don'ts, and offer solutions. As a result, you must initially gain an improved comprehension of these problems and learn about their significance before making a decision based on your abilities and lifestyle and solving it with your suitable techniques and solutions.

Learning and observing management in your life can be facilitated by a sense of purpose and motivation. If you want to obtain an objective in your life and workouts, you will have to control or manage numerous problems. You will seek to correct any shortcomings and manage them in some manner. The only factor that matters is how you handle and manage a shortcoming. It is critical to consider how you will approach and resolve a problem. The principle and foundation of management in an athlete's sports life is, initially, recognizing and understanding the problem and, second, determining how to encounter it.

For an athlete to achieve his ultimate objective, which is triumph and championship, and to be able to achieve the pinnacles of sporting success, he must be able to solve the problems and challenges encountered in his daily life.

Numerous world-class athletes could achieve great achievement simply by adhering to this principle. Due to their failure to address this issue, however, they have encountered significant obstacles in their athletic careers, have been kept away from achieving great achievement, and have been unable to demonstrate their actual abilities. They have unavoidably faded away after flickering like a brilliant and beautiful star.

An athlete should be able to control his surrounding issues and worries when managing his athletic life. To avoid any disruptions in his championship sport, either in sports or in his personal life, he must also appropriately and logically handle them. If you want to be able to deal with these deficiencies rationally and eradicate them, you must increase your sphere of information, knowledge, and insight or acquire this information and knowledge through experience. To traverse this path of ups and downs more conveniently, you need to broaden your sight as much as possible and gain a lot of experience.

As previously stated, you must have a complete package in order to reach the world and Olympic platforms and achievement. Your overall ranking will be determined by the total of these factors. Your rank will be reduced if any of the five wrestling principles are lacking or flawed.

Coaching

Let's give some feedback on the past and discuss the value of sports life management before we discuss the coaching issue. We discussed the significance of an athlete's ability to manage and control their life during their athletic career. As previously stated, if the athlete is unable to manage and control his athletic life, he will most likely not achieve great achievement. As you are aware, you must have a full package in order to achieve success and championship peaks. The management of athletic life was one of these five principles. You were informed that having and achieving the highest level of intelligence and knowledge was a requirement and component of achieving this level of management. Presently, increasing awareness and consciousness or getting experience, ultimately arrive at the same path, which is the comprehension and understanding of an event.

Humans have authority and the ability to make their own decisions. They can decide whether to approach a subject with knowledge, awareness, and insight or whether he would rather experience the subject before accepting it. You have the option of choosing the quicker and safer route, which is awareness enhancement. You may incline to take the more time-consuming and costly route, which is gaining experience. All of this was said to achieve to a conclusion that, as you understand, the path to increasing awareness is much simpler and shorter, and it can lead us to the shores of tranquility much faster and more effectively. But how?

As previously stated, numerous ways exist to obtain data and increase knowledge. This information can be acquired, for instance, through studying, friends and acquaintances, or coaching and a professional advisor. It is essential to find and comprehend the information.

What exactly is coaching?

Coaching encompasses all economic, political, social, cultural, and sporting fields. It has numerous dimensions, but when the word coaching is mentioned in our country, most people's minds immediately turn to sports and coaching.

Coaching, on the other hand, refers to a person who listens to your statements and a questioner who attempts to hear your words thoroughly. He will afterward convey your words to you in a more thorough manner, enabling you to approach a subject more effectively and accurately, eliminate erroneous mental filters, and achieve greater knowledge and insight. An excellent coach is a good leader who, through his instruction, encourages a person to select a better and more correct path so that he can achieve his desired objectives more quickly and efficiently.

The same can be said about sports. A coach can help you get to know yourself better so you can make smarter decisions about yourself and accomplish your objectives.

This implies gaining more knowledge and insight, which will result in your achievement because you will be able to understand and manage problems more quickly and effectively, as well as make more informed decisions.

You can increase your chances of success in achieving your goals by always having a dependable and knowledgeable coach and an excellent consultant. He can steer you from secondary and unreliable routes to achievement and persuade you to the primary and more reliable route, which is the achievement of sports peaks